VIETNAM STUDIES

CEDAR FALLS-JUNCTION CITY: A TURNING POINT

by
Lieutenant General Bernard William Rogers

DEPARTMENT OF THE ARMY
WASHINGTON, D.C., 1974

For sale by the Superintendent of Documents, U.S. Government Printing Office
Washington, D.C. 20402 - Price $2
Stock No. 0820-00477

Library of Congress Catalog Card Number: 73-600007
First Printing

Foreword

The United States Army has met an unusually complex challenge in Southeast Asia. In conjunction with the other services, the Army has fought in support of a national policy of assisting an emerging nation to develop governmental processes of its own choosing, free of outside coercion. In addition to the usual problems of waging armed conflict, the assignment in Southeast Asia has required superimposing the immensely sophisticated tasks of a modern army upon an underdeveloped environment and adapting them to demands covering a wide spectrum. These involved helping to fulfill the basic needs of an agrarian population, dealing with the frustrations of antiguerrilla operations, and conducting conventional campaigns against well-trained and determined regular units.

As this assignment nears an end, the U.S. Army must prepare for other challenges that may lie ahead. While cognizant that history never repeats itself exactly and that no army ever profited from trying to meet a new challenge in terms of the old one, the Army nevertheless stands to benefit immensely from a study of its experience, its shortcomings no less than its achievements.

Aware that some years must elapse before the official histories will provide a detailed and objective analysis of the experience in Southeast Asia, we have sought a forum whereby some of the more salient aspects of that experience can be made available now. At the request of the Chief of Staff, a representative group of senior officers who served in important posts in Vietnam and who still carry a heavy burden of day-to-day responsibilities has prepared a series of monographs. These studies should be of great value in helping the Army develop future operational concepts while at the same time contributing to the historical record and providing the American public with an interim report on the performance of men and officers who have responded, as others have throughout our history, to exacting and trying demands.

The reader should be reminded that most of the writing was accomplished while the war in Vietnam was at its peak, and the monographs frequently refer to events of the past as if they were taking place in the present.

All monographs in the series are based primarily on official

FOREWORD

records, with additional material from published and unpublished secondary works, from debriefing reports and interviews with key participants, and from the personal experience of the author. To facilitate security clearance, annotation and detailed bibliography have been omitted from the published version; a fully documented account with bibliography is filed with the Office of the Chief of Military History.

Lieutenant General Bernard William Rogers is especially well qualified to write *Cedar Falls-Junction City* because of a broad and varied military career. His military experience includes action in Korea and Vietnam as well as assignments in Germany. In Korea he served in the 2d Infantry Division as commander of the 3d Battalion, 9th Infantry, and later joined the staff of the Commander in Chief, United Nations and Far East Commands, in Tokyo, Japan. While assigned to the 24th Infantry Division in Augsburg, Germany, he served as commander of the 1st Battle Group, 19th Infantry, and for fourteen months as chief of staff of the division. In Vietnam he served as assistant division commander of the 1st Infantry Division, where he participated in Operations CEDAR FALLS and JUNCTION CITY.

General Rogers attended Oxford University, England, from 1947 to 1950 as a Rhodes Scholar, receiving the B.A. and M.A. degrees in philosophy, politics, and economics. Later from September 1967 to June 1969 he served as commandant of cadets at the United States Military Academy. He was Chief of Legislative Liaison on the staff of the Secretary of the Army from January 1971 until November 1972. He is currently Deputy Chief of Staff for Personnel, U.S. Army.

Washington, D.C.
15 June 1973

VERNE L. BOWERS
Major General, USA
The Adjutant General

Preface

Cedar Falls-Junction City: A Turning Point has been written at the request of General William C. Westmoreland, Chief of Staff of the Army, who, concerned about the lack of authoritative accounts of various actions and activities in Vietnam, desired that a series of monographs be prepared to fill the void in the Army's historical library.

Operations CEDAR FALLS and JUNCTION CITY took place during the first five months of 1967 and were the first multidivisional operations in Vietnam to be conducted according to a preconceived plan. They were to result in a turning point in the war: they confirmed that such operations do have a place in counterinsurgency warfare today; they brought an end to the enemy's thinking that his third phase of the war—large-scale operations throughout the country—would be successful; they caused the enemy to re-evaluate his tactics and revert to smaller-scale guerrilla operations; they destroyed his camps, pillaged his supplies, and killed hundreds of his best troops; they proved to the enemy that his old sanctuaries were no longer inviolable, thus causing him to depend primarily upon those located over the border in Cambodia; they helped convince the enemy that the maintenance of large bases and main force units near urban areas was risky business; and they enhanced immeasurably the confidence of the allied forces in South Vietnam, a confidence which had been growing since the dark days of the first half of 1965. Thus CEDAR FALLS and JUNCTION CITY were to become the most important operations of the war to that time, and perhaps since.

For the military history buff, Operation CEDAR FALLS will not be nearly so interesting as JUNCTION CITY because it consisted primarily of small unit contacts and the onerous tasks of finding and destroying base camps, storage facilities, and tunnels and of clearing jungles. CEDAR FALLS was unique, however, in that one of its missions was to evacuate some 6,000 inhabitants of the Iron Triangle area and destroy their villages. JUNCTION CITY, on the other hand, was more varied in view of its scope and the fact that there were five battles interspersed among the air assaults and the numerous search and destroy activities.

As an assistant division commander of the 1st Infantry Division

PREFACE

from November 1966 to August 1967, I had the opportunity firsthand to observe and participate in the planning and execution of the two operations. From a personal standpoint, it was an extremely rewarding experience to serve with the Big Red One during the period when its commanding general for CEDAR FALLS was Major General William E. DePuy and for JUNCTION CITY was Major General John H. Hay, Jr. Their intricate planning, rapid and decisive execution of actions, and employment of new concepts, coupled with the bravery and skill of our troops, made these two operations the success they were.

I have expanded this monograph somewhat by including an introduction which covers those major events from the time of our initial commitment in Vietnam to Operation ATTLEBORO in November 1966, events which led to and influenced CEDAR FALLS and JUNCTION CITY. The hope is that the introduction will assist the reader in putting these two operations in perspective.

In assembling the data for this monograph, I have drawn primarily from after action reports and interviews, documented lessons learned, newspaper and magazine articles, personal letters, written and tape-recorded material, and my recollection of events. For the historical information contained in the introduction, I have relied exclusively upon the excellent document, *Report on the War in Vietnam*, by Admiral U. S. Grant Sharp and General William C. Westmoreland.

I would like to thank the members of the Office, Chief of Legislative Liaison, Department of the Army, who have assisted in the compilation of the material for this monograph. I would particularly like to express my appreciation to Lieutenant Colonel John R. Vilas for researching and organizing this document. The final product is mine, and for it I assume full responsibility.

Washington, D.C. BERNARD W. ROGERS
15 June 1973 Lieutenant General, U.S. Army

Contents

	Page
INTRODUCTION	1

PART ONE

CEDAR FALLS, 8–26 January 1967

Chapter
- I. BACKGROUND AND PLANNING 15
- II. POSITIONING THE ANVIL—OPERATIONS FITCHBURG AND NIAGARA FALLS 25
  - 25th Infantry Division 25
  - 1st Infantry Division 27
- III. D-DAY—BEN SUC 30
  - 25th Infantry Division 30
  - 1st Infantry Division 31
  - Ben Suc Village 31
  - The Initial Assault 34
- IV. PHASE II—THE HAMMER SWINGS 42
  - 3d Brigade 42
  - Task Force Deane 44
  - 25th Infantry Division 46
  - Small Unit Actions 46
- V. THE HAMMER STRIKES 51
  - 25th Infantry Division 51
  - 1st Infantry Division 55
- VI. ENGINEER AND CHEMICAL OPERATIONS 60
  - Bridge on the Thi Tinh 61
  - Jungle Clearing Operations 61
  - Tunnel Exploration and Destruction 66

Chapter	Page
The Engineer Navy	70
Chemical Operations	71
VII. THE RESULTS	74

PART TWO

JUNCTION CITY, 22 February–14 May 1967

VIII. PLANNING AND PREPARATION	83
IX. THE WARM-UP TOSSES: GADSDEN AND TUCSON	91
Operation Gadsden	91
Operation Tucson	94
X. PHASE I—THE HORSESHOE IS PITCHED	97
Combat Forces	97
D-Day, 22 February 1967	101
D Plus 1, 23 February	103
D Plus 2, 24 February	104
End of Phase I, 25 February–17 March	106
XI. THE BATTLES OF PREK KLOK	112
Prek Klok I	112
Prek Klok II	117
XII. PHASE II—EAST TO WEST	122
XIII. THE BATTLES OF AP BAU BANG II, SUOI TRE, AND AP GU	129
Ap Bau Bang II	129
Suoi Tre	135
Ap Gu	140
XIV. PHASE III—TERMINATION	149
EPILOGUE	154
GLOSSARY	161
INDEX	165

Chart

No.		Page
1.	Communist Party Dominance in Enemy Organization	3

Maps

No.		Page
1.	Corps Tactical Zones, Republic of Vietnam	xii
2.	Major Battles Near Saigon, 1966	6
3.	War Zones	8
4.	ATTLEBORO (Operational Area)	9
5.	The Iron Triangle and CEDAR FALLS Operational Area	16
6.	CEDAR FALLS (Concept of Operations)	20
7.	CEDAR FALLS (D-Day, D + 1)	32
8.	War Zone C	88
9.	Operation GADSDEN, 3–21 February 1967	92
10.	Operation TUCSON (Concept of Operations)	94
11.	Operation JUNCTION CITY (Phase I)	98
12.	The Battle of Prek Klok I, 28 February 1967	113
13.	The Battle of Prek Klok II, 10 March 1967	118
14.	JUNCTION CITY (Concept, Phase II)	125
15.	The Battle of Ap Bau Bang, 20 March 1967	130
16.	Battle of Suoi Tre, 21 March 1967	136
17.	Battle of Ap Gu, 1 April 1967	141

Illustrations

	Page
Elements of the 173d Airborne Brigade Arrive in Saigon From Okinawa, 1965	4
105-mm. Howitzer Lifted Into Position by Chinook During Operation BIRMINGHAM	7
105-mm. Howitzer Crew Fires in Support of the 1st Infantry Division	10
Brigadier General Bernard W. Rogers Directs His Troops in Battle by Radio	22
Armored Personnel Carriers Move Through Scrub Jungle	26
Brigadier General John R. Deane, Jr., Checks the Location of a Patrol	28
Private First Class Willie Foxworth Takes a Position Behind Weathered Graves	36
First Sergeant George L. Taylor Inspects Captured Enemy Mortar Rounds	43
Members of the 503d Infantry and 11th Armored Cavalry in Thanh Dien Forest	45
Members of Company C, 1st Battalion, 27th Infantry, Patrolling the Saigon River	53

	Page
Tankers from the 1st Squadron, 4th Cavalry, in a Rubber Plantation	56
American and Vietnamese Soldiers Assist Refugees	58
Rome Plow in Operation	62
Preparing Landing Zone	63
Engineers Rappelling off Helicopter	64
Inspecting an Enemy Booby Trap	65
Searching for Tunnels	66
Flamethrower in Action	72
Combined Arms at Work in the Iron Triangle	75
American Adviser and Vietnamese Soldiers Keeping Watch on Viet Cong Captives	76
Infantrymen Move Through Heavy Brush Near the Michelin Plantation	95
Individual Ammunition Issue	102
Elements of the 11th Armored Cavalry Regiment Guarding Road to Rubber Plantation	104
Moving Through the Jungle	105
Hacking Out a Trail	107
Company Sweep in War Zone	108
An Infantryman Returns Fire During an Enemy Attack	109
First Leiutenant Edward Christiansen Calls for Air Strikes Over a Suspected Viet Cong Position	117
Guiding a Recovery Vehicle Across a River	124
A Huey Prepares To Land Near Awaiting Troops	126
Infantrymen Dash From Helicopters To Move Against Enemy Forces	147
Dropping Supplies North of Tay Ninh City	150
Armored Personnel Carriers Piled High With Captured Rice	152

All illustrations are from Department of the Army files.

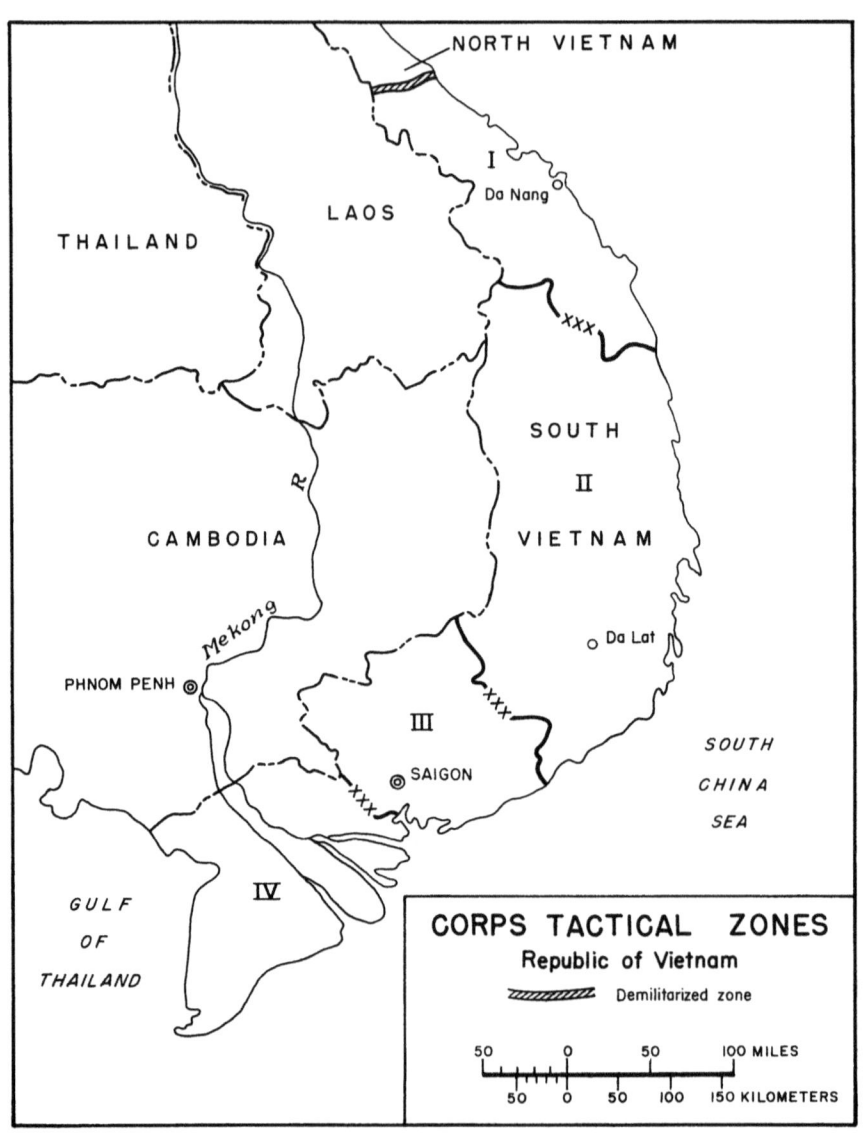

MAP 1

Introduction

The war in Vietnam is as highly complex as any in our country's history. It is a war with no front, no rear. There is often no easily identifiable enemy. The Communists deny that there are any North Vietnamese in the south. Those from the south live among the very persons they threaten. At the same time we engage multibattalion forces we also fight against individual guerrilla bands numbering but a few men. (*Map 1*)

We have been facing a Communist aggressor whose avowed objective is to gain control of the government, the land, and the peoples of South Vietnam. We have agreed to support the South Vietnamese against the enemy in order to buy time for the south, time in which the people can prepare to defend themselves and to shape their own destiny.

We are engaged in a conflict in which we are allied with forces whose approach to life is different from ours and whose history goes back centuries before ours. Using sophisticated weapons in the hands of tough, well-trained American soldiers, we, along with our allies, have been fighting a dedicated and disciplined enemy in South Vietnam who employs no air power, little naval effort, and comparatively few mechanized vehicles. Yet he has forced us, the most powerful nation in the world, to fight the longest war in our history.

This monograph concerns two operations conducted in early 1967 which marked a turning point in this conflict from the viewpoint of the tide of battle and tactical doctrine. The conditions which led to this turning point had been developing over the years from the time of the withdrawal of the French from Indochina in 1954 until Operation ATTLEBORO in late 1966.

At the outset of this twelve-year period the United States endorsed the new Geneva Accords and offered, through President Dwight D. Eisenhower, "to assist the Government of Vietnam in developing and maintaining a strong, viable state, capable of resisting attempted subversion or aggression through military means" in the hope "that such aid, combined with . . . continuing efforts, will contribute effectively toward an independent Vietnam endowed with a strong government." From this commitment stems our involvement in South Vietnam.

Following this commitment by our Commander in Chief in

October 1954, the U.S. involvement in South Vietnam grew: a Military Assistance Advisory Group (later becoming the U.S. Military Assistance Command, Vietnam) to organize, train, and equip the armed forces of South Vietnam was established; helicopter companies to support the Vietnamese Army were deployed; combat and logistical airlift support was provided to South Vietnamese forces; Special Forces detachments were introduced, followed by the 5th Special Forces Group; U.S. tactical aircraft were deployed to South Vietnam and used in close air support; B-52 bombers were employed; and the deployment to South Vietnam of U.S. Army and Marine ground forces along with supporting air and naval forces was accelerated commencing in mid-1965. By the end of 1966 U.S. military forces in South Vietnam numbered 385,000 men.

Necessitating this increasing commitment of U.S. forces and resources to South Vietnam between 1954 and 1966 was the concomitant growth in the size and quality of Viet Cong and North Vietnamese forces in the south. The Communist Viet Minh had left many cadres in the south in 1954 which were grouped into a political-paramilitary organization under orders of Hanoi. This organization, known as the Viet Cong, was infused with large numbers of "regroupees" who had gone north between 1954-1955, received intensive political and military training, and returned to the south as cadres and leaders for the Viet Cong units and infrastructure. Pursuing initially a policy of subversion, espionage, and terror, this organization would turn to intensified guerrilla warfare, culminating in the employment of large military units. By 1960 some battalion-size units had been formed, and in later years Viet Cong military activity was conducted more and more by larger forces. By 1964 regular North Vietnamese Army units were starting to be deployed into South Vietnam to begin what Hanoi anticipated would be the final and decisive phase of the war. In that same year the enemy began to convert from weapons of various calibers and origins to a standard family of small arms. By the end of 1966 the total combat strength of the enemy was over 280,000 plus an additional 80,000 political cadre.

Tying together the various elements of the insurgency in South Vietnam was the Lao Dong (Worker's) Party regional committee for South Vietnam—the Central Office of South Vietnam (COSVN). All the various elements of the Communist organization in the south, military and civil, were and are responsive to directions from this office. Providing the administrative apparatus—the so-called Viet Cong shadow government—was the National Libera-

CHART 1—COMMUNIST PARTY DOMINANCE IN ENEMY ORGANIZATION*

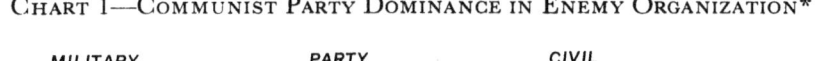

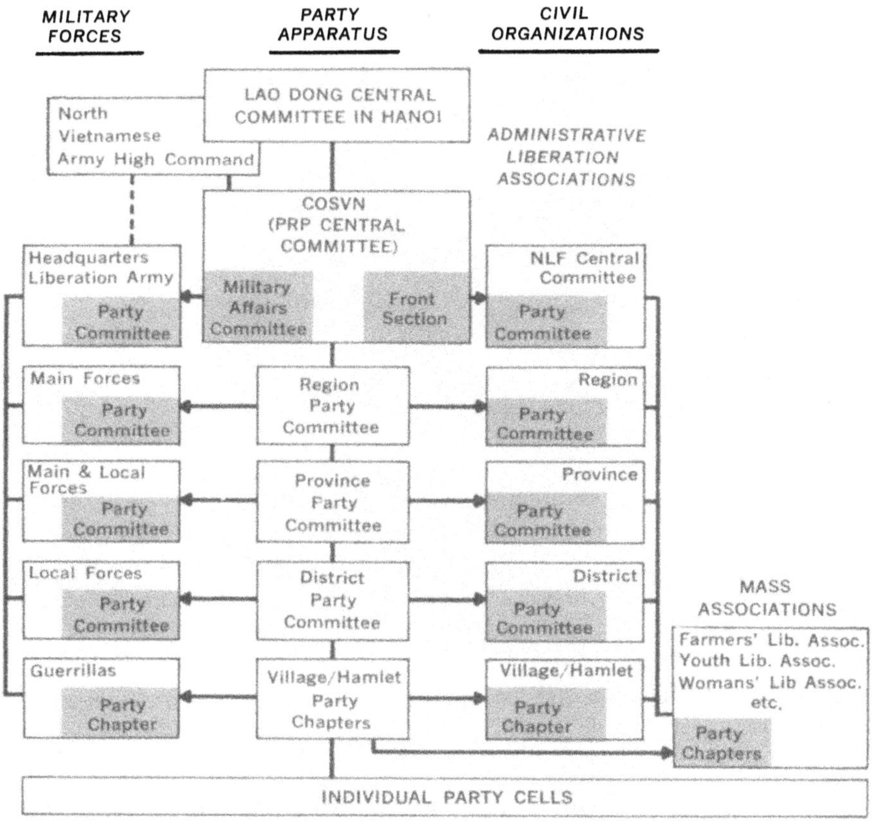

* This chart shows the relationship between the major elements of the enemy organization. Although the military and civilian elements are portrayed as separate entities—with the military and civilian headquarters controlling each echelon of their organization directly—their real organizational substance came from, and was irrevocably tied to, the party. The arrows leading left and right from each level of the party apparatus indicate the true lines of control.

tion Front. All was controlled by the Lao Dong Central Committee in Hanoi. (*Chart 1*)

Impacting considerably upon the developments of the period 1954–1966 was the political situation within South Vietnam. Throughout the countryside the acts of terror by the Viet Cong resulted in the assassination and kidnapping of many government officials and supporters. By the spring of 1963 President Ngo Dinh Diem was being accused of provoking an adverse reaction among the people. Especially were the Buddhists unhappy. Demonstrations, immolations, and turmoil followed. Finally, on 1 November 1963, Diem was overthrown and assassinated. There followed a

ELEMENTS OF THE 173D AIRBORNE BRIGADE ARRIVE IN SAIGON FROM OKINAWA. 1965

period of political instability which featured many coups and countercoups with military and political factions vying for political power with each other and within their own organizations. The effectiveness of the government deteriorated; governmental institutions founded under Diem began to disappear. The impact of this instability was felt at every echelon of political authority in the south. The Viet Cong's position throughout the country grew stronger as that of the government declined. It was not until mid-1965 that any sort of stability was injected into the Saigon political scene, this occurring when General Nguyen Van Thieu was proclaimed chief of state and Air Vice- Marshal Nguyen Cao Ky was installed as premier. The Thieu–Ky government remained in power, and these two leaders were inaugurated in 1967 for a four-year term as president and vice-president, respectively.

From the termination of the French involvement in Indochina in 1954 until Operation ATTLEBORO in 1966, the tactics and employment of troops by the two sides underwent considerable changes.

Until about 1960 the Viet Cong employed small units on missions of terror: assassinations, kidnappings, destruction. In 1960 the first battalion-size attacks were conducted by the Viet Cong; by 1961 the attacks had increased in frequency and had expanded to multibattalion. To counter the growing insurgency the South Vietnam government set about increasing its regular military forces, its paramilitary forces, and its pacification program. The combined U.S.–South Vietnamese effort seemed to be leading to a shifting of the tide of battle by the end of 1962; however, with the growing political turmoil in the spring of 1963 followed in November by the overthrow of Diem, the bottom fell out of the military efforts of the South Vietnamese forces. Many of the government's strategic hamlets were lost, weapons losses increased, and many local paramilitary units simply faded away.

By 1964 Viet Cong battalions were growing into regiments and regiments into divisions. Battles were won by both sides during the year, culminating with the Viet Cong 9th Division's seizure of the Catholic village of Binh Gia east of Saigon on 28 December. During the battle the division ambushed and destroyed a South Vietnamese Ranger battalion and a Marine battalion. This battle was a major event for both sides. The enemy considered it the beginning of the final "mobile" phase of the war, and the South Vietnamese saw it as the beginning of a military challenge they could not meet alone.

The year 1965 saw the first commitment of regular North Vietnamese Army forces in South Vietnam with their apparent intention of cutting the country in half. By late spring of 1965 the South Vietnamese Army was losing about one infantry battalion and one district capital a week to the enemy. It was then that U.S. ground forces were requested and, starting in July, began to arrive in substantial numbers. By August 1965 U.S. forces were being committed to combat, but in less than division strength. By the end of the year the Viet Cong 9th Division was heard from again as its 272d Regiment overran the South Vietnamese 7th Regiment in the Michelin Plantation.

1966 was a year of accelerated buildup and development and the beginning of major offensive operations by U.S. and South Vietnamese forces. There was a number of allied operations during the year, but the ones of concern to us were those conducted near Saigon and in the major enemy areas near the capital such as in the Iron Triangle and in War Zones C and D. In April 1966, Operation ABILENE took place east of Saigon as a spoiling operation against an enemy move on the capital. (*Map 2*) In the same month

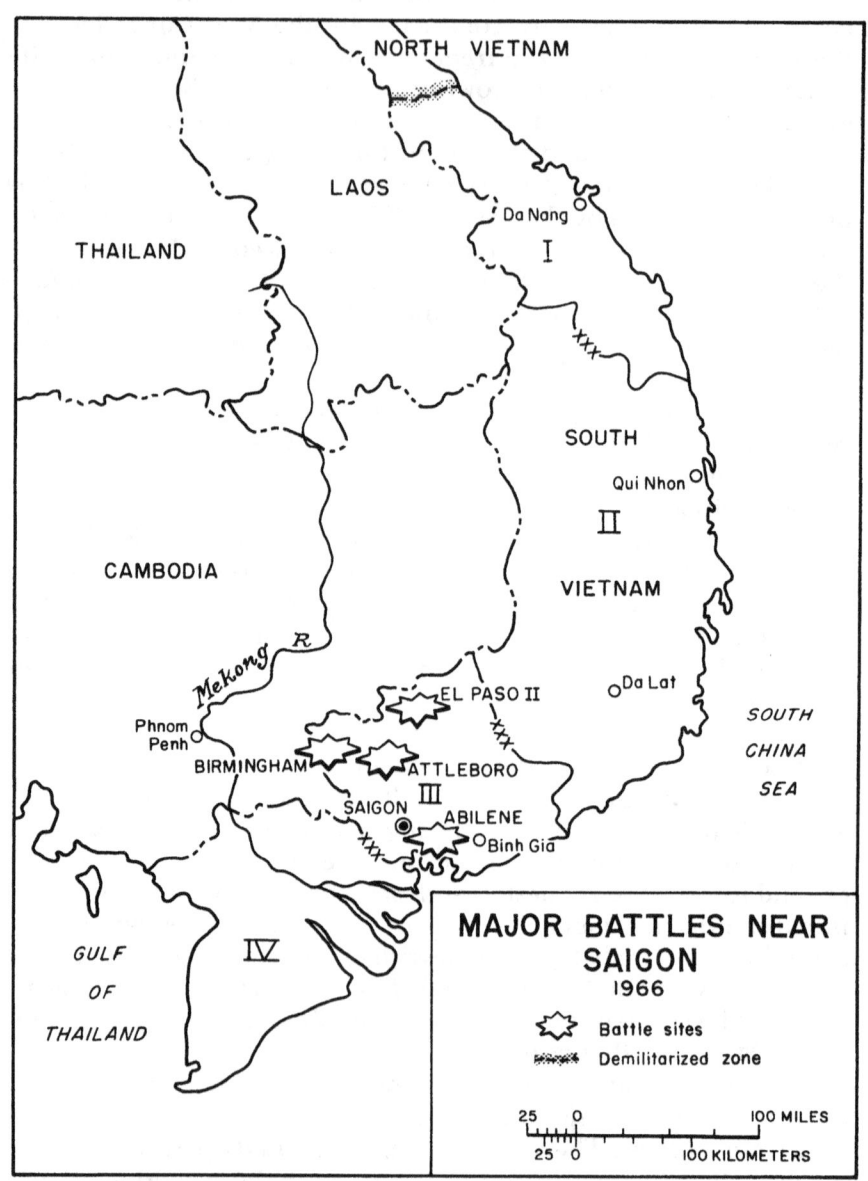

MAP 2

A 105-MM. HOWITZER IS LIFTED INTO POSITION *by a CH-47 "Chinook" helicopter during Operation Birmingham.*

Operation BIRMINGHAM, a move by the U.S. 1st Infantry Division into War Zone C, uncovered great quantities of supplies. In June and July the U.S. 1st Infantry Division and the Vietnamese 5th Division conducted a series of operations, EL PASO II, on the eastern flank of War Zone C in order to open Route 13 from Saigon to the major rubber plantations to the north, as well as to attack the Viet Cong 9th Division massing near the province capital of An Loc. Viet Cong losses were heavy. The 9th Division withdrew after that action into sanctuaries along the Cambodian border in War Zone C. (*Map 3*) In late October 1966 this same division deployed its three regiments along with another North Vietnamese Army regiment into central Tay Ninh Province for the purpose of attacking the Special Forces camp at Suoi Da with one regiment while ambushing relieving forces with the other regiments. At the same time the recently arrived U.S. 196th Light Infantry Brigade was operating in the same area in search of rice and other enemy supplies.

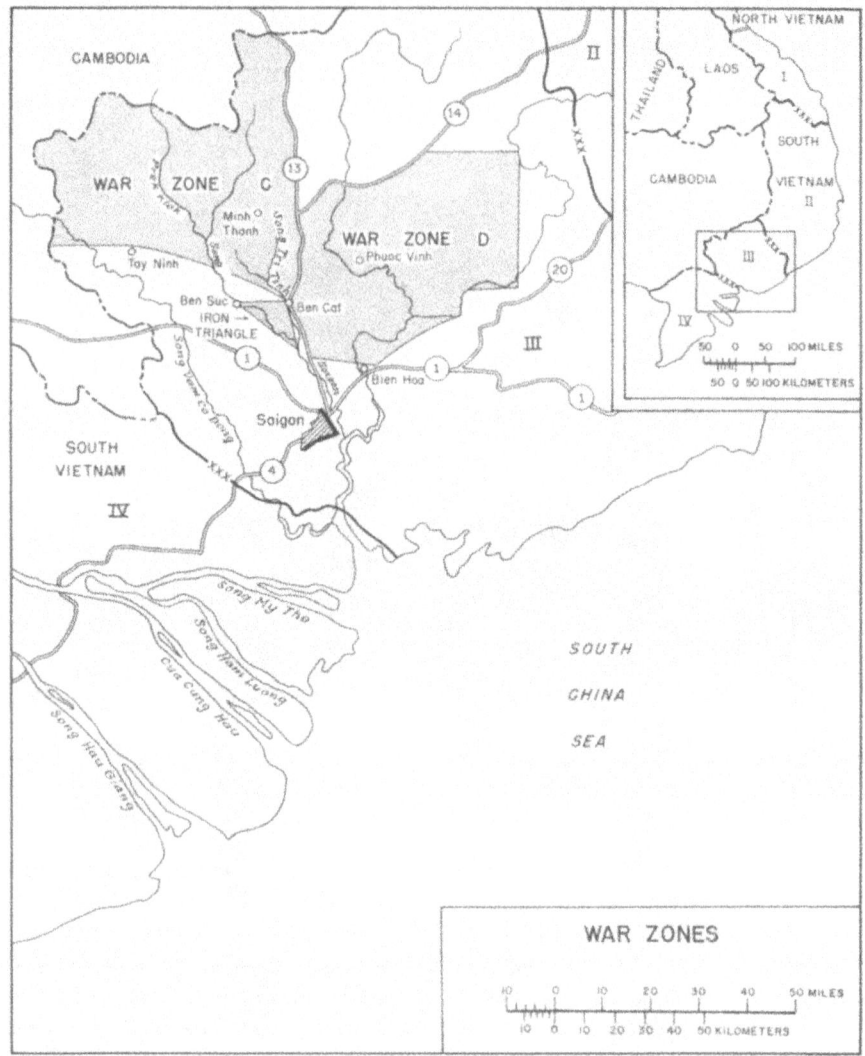

MAP 3

The stage was now set for Operation ATTLEBORO.

ATTLEBORO was to be a search and destroy operation conducted by the 196th Light Infantry Brigade in an area generally described as a rectangle twenty kilometers wide by sixty kilometers long located east and north of Tay Ninh city. (*Map 4*) The operation was initiated by the 196th on 14 September 1966 with the airmobile assault of a single battalion followed by a search and destroy opera-

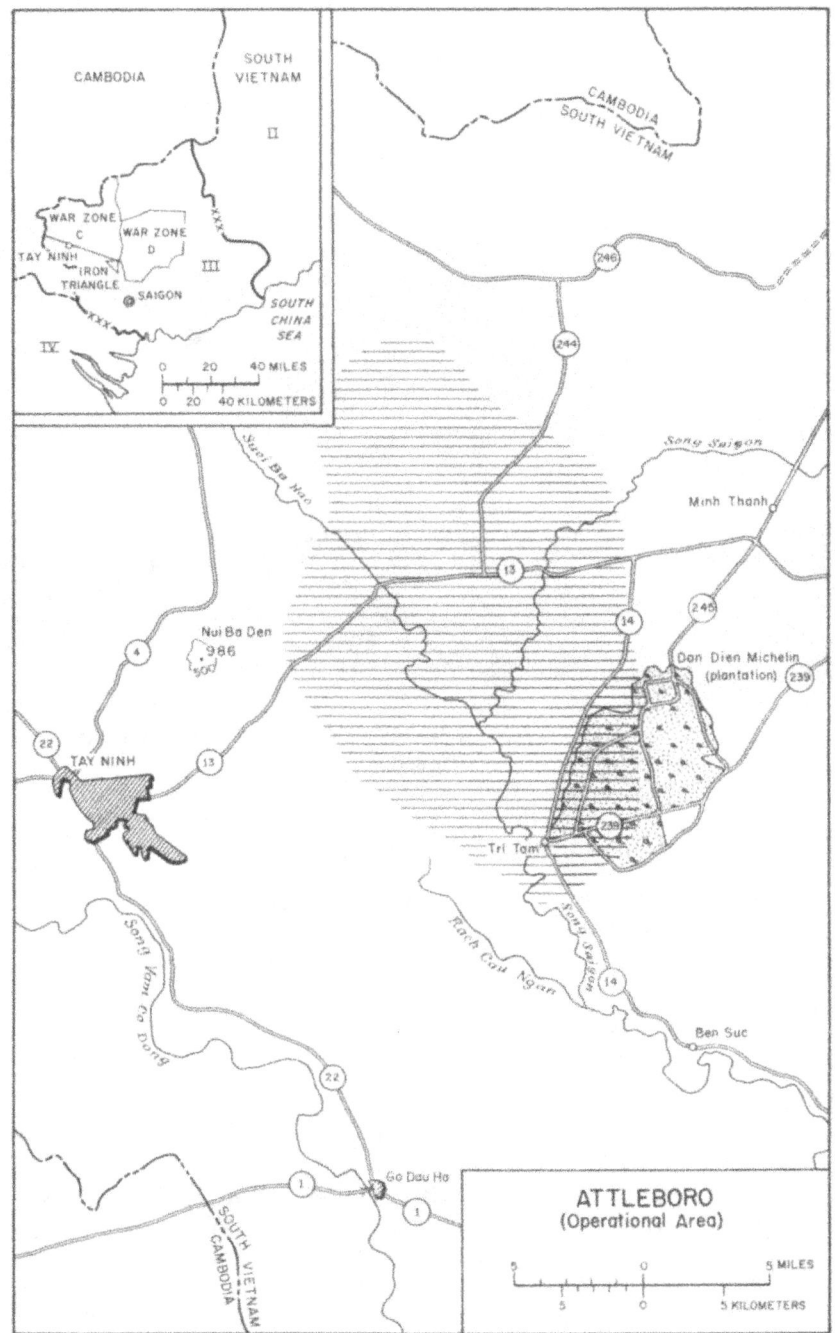

A 105-MM. HOWITZER CREW OF A BATTERY, 2D BATTALION, 33D ARTILLERY, *fires in support of the 1st Infantry Division*

tion of but a few days in which only two significant contacts with the enemy were made. After the initial assault battalion was committed elsewhere, another battalion of the 196th continued the mission from 18 to 24 September; it made no significant contact. It, too, was diverted to another area but returned to ATTLEBORO on 6 October and conducted search and destroy operations for ten more days. During this time the battalion destroyed tunnel complexes, trenches, and fighting positions and captured two tons of rice, many documents, and some enemy arms. It was not until mid-October, as the result of a decision taken at the Military Assistance Command commanders' conference, that ATTLEBORO was expanded to a multibattalion operation with the 196th committing two battalions to its search and destroy activities. Through the end of October action was light and sporadic with no major contact. In fact, the action was so light that between 4 October and 1 November only two immediate air strikes were called in to support the operation.

Meanwhile, the Viet Cong 9th Division was starting to stir again. After its beating in EL PASO II in June and July 1966, the 9th had withdrawn to its sanctuaries deep in War Zone C next to the Cambodian border and had retrained, re-equipped, and absorbed replacements. The plan of the 9th was to use these bases to launch a winter offensive against objectives in Tay Ninh Province. Among its objectives was to be the Special Forces camp at Suoi Da, located twelve kilometers northeast of Tay Ninh city in the shadow of Nui Ba Den, the Black Virgin Mountain, which rose, as if by mistake, some three thousand feet above the surrounding plain. The division also hoped to lure some allied forces into the area in response to an attack by one of its regiments so that these forces might be ambushed by the remaining regiments of the 9th. By late October the regiments assigned to the 9th Viet Cong Division—the 271st, 272d, 273d, and the 101st North Vietnamese Regiment—had commenced deploying in War Zone C. On 28 October elements of the U.S. 1st Infantry Division made contact with a battalion of the 273d just east of the ATTLEBORO operational area. The commanding officer of one of the companies of the 101st North Vietnamese Army Regiment, captured on 8 November, revealed that his regiment had left its base area on the Cambodian border about 1 November to move south along the eastern boundary of the ATTLEBORO area toward resupply camps.

Sweeping operations by American units near Dau Tieng on 31 October uncovered a major enemy supply base. On 1 November ATTLEBORO became a brigade-size operation with the 196th Brigade assuming operational control of a battalion from the 25th Division. Two days later an airmobile assault by this battalion made contact with elements of the 9th Viet Cong Division; on the same day, 3 November, elements of the U.S. 5th Special Forces Group's mobile strike force, which had been inserted into landing zones near Suoi Da, were also engaged by forces of the 9th Division. Operation ATTLEBORO was about to erupt.

By 5 November it was apparent that a very large enemy force was involved; operational control was initially passed to Major General William E. DePuy, Commanding General, U.S. 1st Infantry Division, and subsequently to the commanding general of II Field Force. Before the operation ended on 24 November, the 1st Division, elements of the U.S. 4th and 25th Infantry Divisions, the 173d Airborne Brigade, and several South Vietnamese Army battalions were committed to it, over 22,000 U.S. and allied troops in all. It was the largest U.S. operation of the war to that time.

It was not only the number of U.S. and allied troops eventually involved which made ATTLEBORO a large operation. There was also during November a total of over 1,600 close air support sorties flown, expending nearly 12,000 tons of ordnance (225 were B–52 sorties carrying 4,000 tons). Cargo aircraft flew 3,300 sorties in transporting 8,900 tons of cargo and 11,500 passengers during the period 18 October–26 November. The enemy left 1,106 dead on the battlefield and had 44 captured. (Friendly losses were 155 killed and 494 wounded.) Later military intelligence reports confirmed the high casualties sustained by the enemy, listing 2,130 killed—including over 1,000 by air strikes, almost 900 wounded, and over 200 missing or captured. Headquarters of the Central Office of South Vietnam was reported struck by B–52 bombers on more than one occasion with the destruction of great quantities of supplies, equipment, and documents. Four Viet Cong battalion commanders and 5 company commanders were reported killed in the operation.

Not only would its casualties pose a serious problem to the Viet Cong 9th Division, so too would the pillaging of its depot area by U.S. and South Vietnamese forces. Over 2,000 tons of rice were captured, as were many tons of salt, 19,000 grenades, 500 claymore mines, and many individual and crew-served weapons. Uncovered and destroyed were regimental and battalion headquarters sites, a mine factory, and a vast tunnel complex containing immense quantities of supplies ranging from bolts of cloth to weighing scales. As General DePuy commented, "It is the largest haul we've made."

Hurting from the whipping it had taken, the 9th Division once again disappeared into its sanctuaries to lick its wounds, regroup, and reorganize. It would not be seen on the field of combat again until the spring of 1967.

Operation ATTLEBORO introduced the large-scale, multiorganization operation to the war, albeit as an accident, in response to the Viet Cong 9th Division's Tay Ninh campaign. But ATTLEBORO proved that, within a matter of hours, well-trained and professionally led organizations with proper logistic support could deploy large numbers of battalions to an active operational area and commit those battalions to immediate combat against a highly disciplined enemy. It proved that large-scale operations, perhaps involving the majority of the forces available in corps zone, have a place in modern counterinsurgency warfare and can effectively destroy large enemy forces and equipment and neutralize major base areas. However, the next time such large forces were used in a single operation, it would not be by accident, as CEDAR FALLS and JUNCTION CITY were soon to verify.

PART ONE

CEDAR FALLS, 8–26 JANUARY 1967

CHAPTER I

Background and Planning

Shortly after the completion of Operation BIRMINGHAM in May 1966, General William C. Westmoreland, Commander, U.S. Military Assistance Command, Vietnam, directed Lieutenant General Jonathan O. Seaman, Commanding General, II Field Force, Vietnam, to plan an operation for War Zone C in northern Tay Ninh Province to start soon after the Christmas and New Year standdowns of 1966–67. (*Map 5*) He further indicated that it should be a "big operation." Over the next several months the operation, to be known as JUNCTION CITY, was planned. As approved by General Westmoreland, the operation was to start on 8 January 1967, was to be multidivisional, and was to include a parachute assault. The operation to commence on 8 January would not be JUNCTION CITY: the pre-emptor was to be known as CEDAR FALLS.

As II Field Force troop strength built up in 1966 and it became more capable of attacking the enemy in longtime havens, General Seaman's headquarters was considering the possibility of a powerful strike into the Iron Triangle. The Iron Triangle is generally defined on the southwest by the Saigon River, on the east by the Thi Tinh River, and on the north by a line running west from Ben Cat to the town of Ben Suc on the Saigon River. To the north lies the Thanh Dien Forestry Reserve. The Iron Triangle has been characterized as a dagger pointed at Saigon and, being only twenty kilometers away, was the enemy's largest haven close to that city. The area was heavily fortified and known to contain the Viet Cong headquarters for Military Region IV which directed military, political, and terrorist activities in the Saigon–Gia Dinh capital region complex. Viet Cong control of the Iron Triangle permitted the enemy forces to dominate key transportation routes in the surrounding area. This important center for controlling and supporting enemy operations had to be attacked decisively and in force if the attack were to succeed in rupturing and neutralizing the control structure.

At a planning meeting in September 1966 General Seaman discussed the possibility of an operation in the triangle with General Westmoreland, who suggested a co-ordinated operation with forces

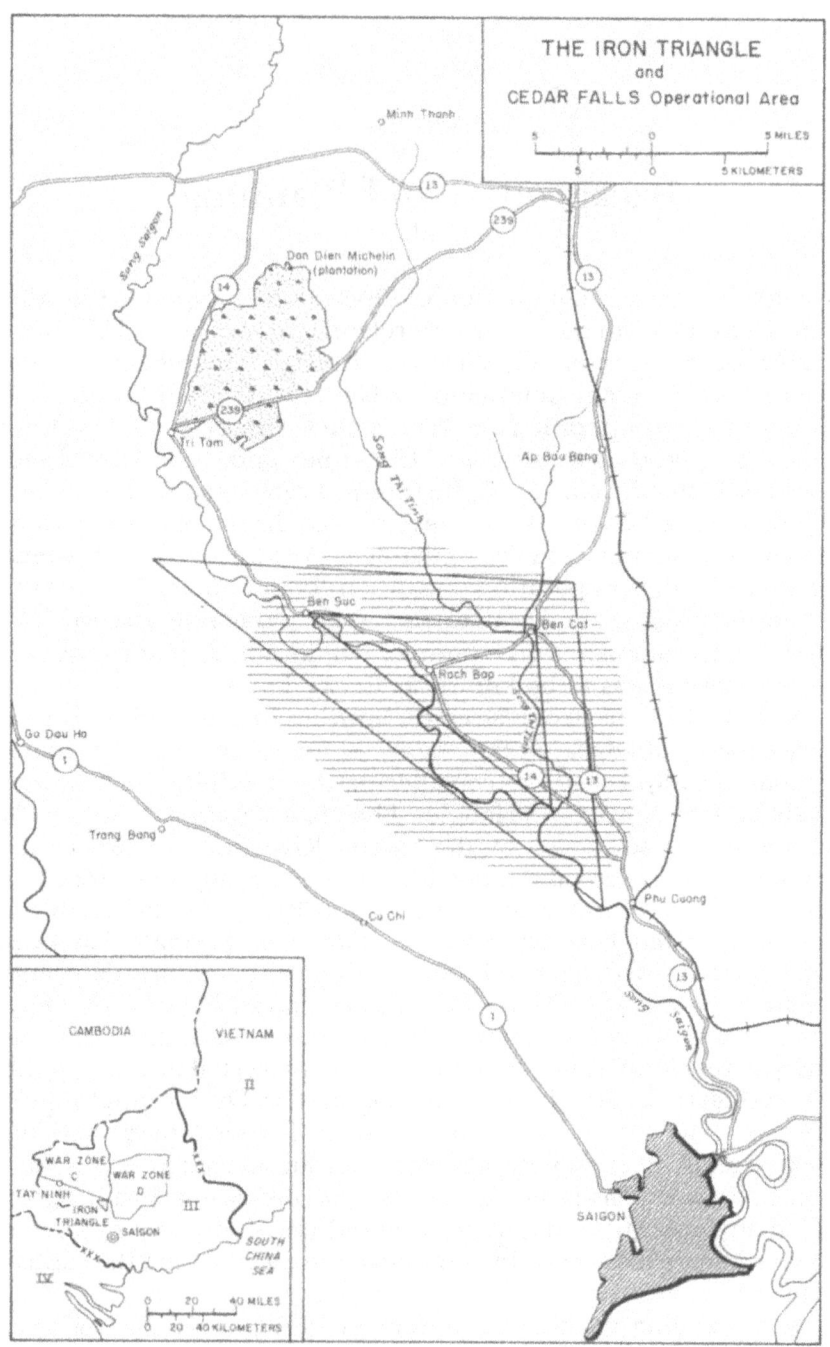

MAP 5

on both sides of the Saigon River. He envisioned troops moving into position on one side of the river to form an anvil followed by a rapid move from the other side to hammer the enemy against the anvil. Discussion also turned to the need for extensive clearing to strip the area and deprive the enemy of concealment. By November General Seaman's headquarters was planning not only for Operation JUNCTION CITY but also for CEDAR FALLS. Intelligence collection was directed at both operations.

A new approach to assigning intelligence collection responsibilities in III Corps had been taken with the publication of a II Field Force, Vietnam, intelligence collection plan. The plan assigned specific intelligence collection areas, tasks, and responsibilities to U.S. and allied units within the III Corps area; the objective was a closely integrated and co-ordinated effort by U.S. and allied agencies. Unit collection responsibilities were assigned on the basis of geographic areas. Close liaison was effected between U.S. and allied units from division through battalion level and between U.S. advisers and corresponding commanders of South Vietnamese Army units or province and district chiefs. The plan was designed to provide for the collection of maximum information with minimum duplication of effort.

A step was also taken to improve the intelligence collection effort through the establishment of a source control program in the III Corps area. When fully implemented, this program administratively controlled and identified confidential informants and sources, assisted in their evaluation, prevented utilization of each source by more than one agency, and avoided employment of unreliable agents.

Operation CEDAR FALLS was the first large-scale operation to benefit from "pattern activity analysis," a system begun in mid-1966. This procedure consisted of detailed plotting on maps of information on enemy activity obtained from a variety of sources over an extended period of time. As more data were plotted, patterns of activity and locations emerged. It thereby became possible to focus prime attention on those areas of intensive or unusual activity.

Aerial observation and photography, sensors, patrol reports, infrared devices, sampan traffic counts, enemy probes of Regional and Popular Forces posts, agent reports, civilian movement reports, reports of increased antiaircraft fire, disclosures of caches (and the amount and nature of the material in them), and captured documents—these sources and more revealed much about enemy intentions. Increases in road ambushes or bridge destruction usually meant that the Viet Cong intended to attack in a location where denial of the roads would aid the enemy. Some idea of the enemy's intent could be determined by checking even the amount of wood shipped into an area for making caskets or the number of civilians impressed as porters. The extent and nature of the enemy's own intelligence gathering revealed much about his intentions and even the size of the operation he was planning.

Detailed plotting of all this information and careful analysis of the patterns enabled U.S. forces to launch spoiling attacks both with ground troops and with massive air strikes. Where no pronounced pattern developed in an area, efforts were concentrated elsewhere, thereby conserving forces. Pattern activity analysis was invaluable in developing broad long-range direction of military operations, while at lower echelons it provided commanders a basis for planning day-by-day operations.

The excellence of the intelligence effort was vividly demonstrated by the results achieved. A comparison of installations discovered during Operation CEDAR FALLS with order-of-battle intelligence holdings collected before the operation disclosed a high degree of correlation. For example, of 177 separate enemy facilities found by the 11th Armored Cavalry Regiment, 156, or 88.1 percent, were located within 500 meters of the locations previously reported. The average distance was about 200 meters.

Intelligence information prompted General Seaman to recommend that Operation CEDAR FALLS precede JUNCTION CITY. General Seaman related the events surrounding the change as follows:

> In early December, if I recall correctly, I received a telephone call from [Brigadier] General [Joseph A.] McChristian, (Assistant Chief of Staff, Intelligence [J-2], MACV) saying that he would like to come out and brief me on some intelligence information he had concerning the III Corps Tactical Zone. He came out with several young MI (Military Intelligence) lieutenants who had been in some building in Saigon poring over (special) research reports, clandestine reports, and everything else available. The briefing lasted a couple of hours and was a most convincing presentation in that they had a pretty good idea where Military Region IV headquarters was, plus some of the support elements of Military Region IV. General McChristian said he wanted to bring this to my attention for whatever I felt should be done. I did a lot of thinking about all this and was convinced that he had some good solid, sound information. I called my staff in and told them to prepare plans for an operation to seal off the southwest side of the Saigon River and the Iron Triangle with the objective of seeing what we could find with respect to Military Region IV. We came up with a plan of operation that, to me, was pretty sound. I asked General Westmoreland to come to my headquarters so that I could brief him on a concept of operations for "Cedar Falls." We had developed a good cover plan so that we

wouldn't compromise the operation. I was going to propose to him that we postpone "Junction City" for two main reasons.

First, I felt that the intelligence information we received from General McChristian and his people was so good that we had to capitalize on it. Secondly, the 9th Division was on its way from Fort Riley and would arrive in theater in December and early January.

So, I felt that if we postponed "Junction City" for a month or a little more, this would give me another division I could use to take over some of the other missions that were going on. Remember, we didn't conduct just one operation at a time. . . . With those two facts in mind; intelligence, and that the 9th Division was on its way over, I felt that there was a great advantage in postponing "Junction City."

General Westmoreland was briefed on CEDAR FALLS; the advantages and disadvantages were weighed and the decision made: Operation CEDAR FALLS, rather than JUNCTION CITY, would begin on 8 January 1967. The mission: II Field Force, Vietnam, attacks the Iron Triangle and the Thanh Dien Forestry Reserve to destroy enemy forces, infrastructure, installations, and Military Region IV headquarters; evacuates civilian population; and establishes the Iron Triangle as a specified strike zone to preclude its further use as a support base for Viet Cong operations.

General Seaman furnished further planning guidance: the Iron Triangle area was to be attacked violently and decisively with all forces available in a "hammer and anvil" operation. Deceptive deployments on seemingly routine operations would pre-position the forces. The anvil would be positioned first and the hammer then swung through the Iron Triangle. The objective area was to be sealed tightly throughout the operation to prevent enemy escape. The triangle itself was to be scoured for enemy installations, cleared of all civilians, stripped of concealment, and declared a specified strike zone. The destruction of the enemy's Military Region IV headquarters was the principal objective of the operation. (*Map 6*)

In addition to the Military Region IV headquarters, the other Viet Cong units in the area were suspected to be the 272d Regiment, the 1st and 7th Battalions of Military Region IV under the 165th Viet Cong Regiment, the Phu Loi Local Force Battalion, plus three local force companies. (Although the suspected location of the 272d Regiment presented a threat during the initial stages of the operation, this unit displaced to the north as the operation progressed.) Other intelligence sources indicated the 2d, 3d, and 8th Battalions of the 165th Viet Cong Regiment might also be encountered.

The Thanh Dien forest and the Iron Triangle were known to

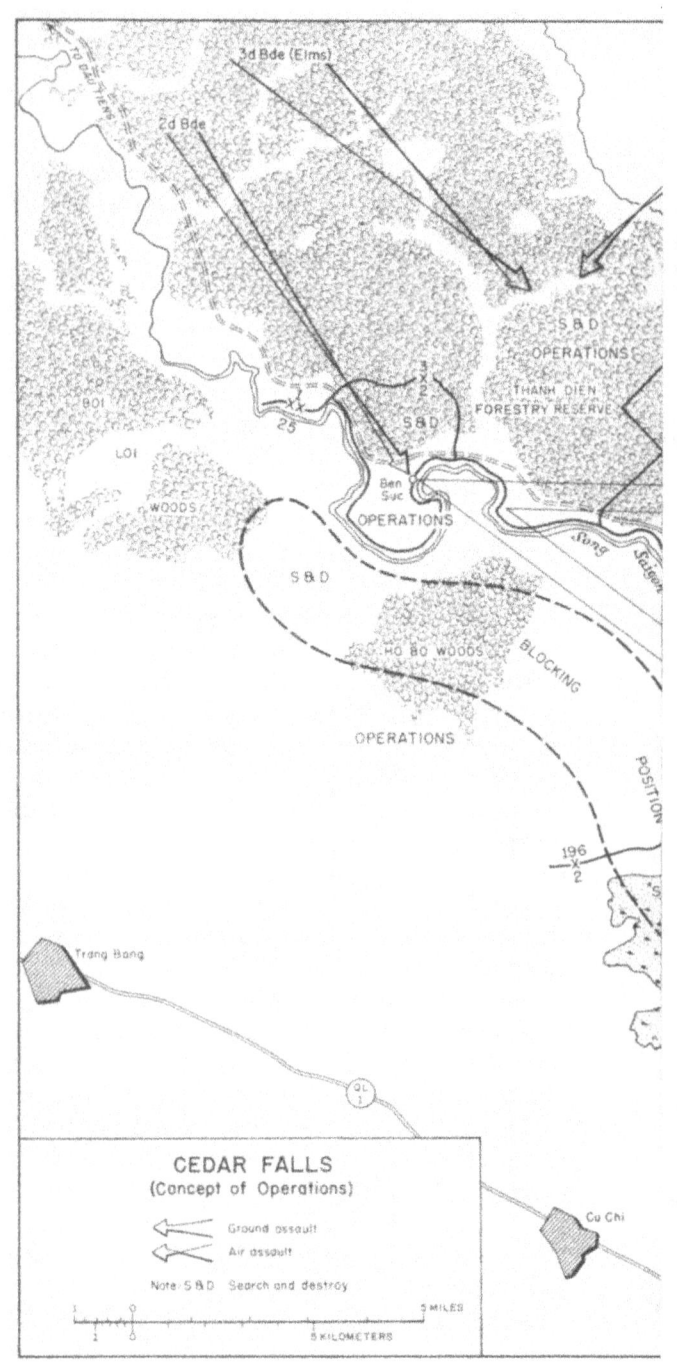

MAP 6

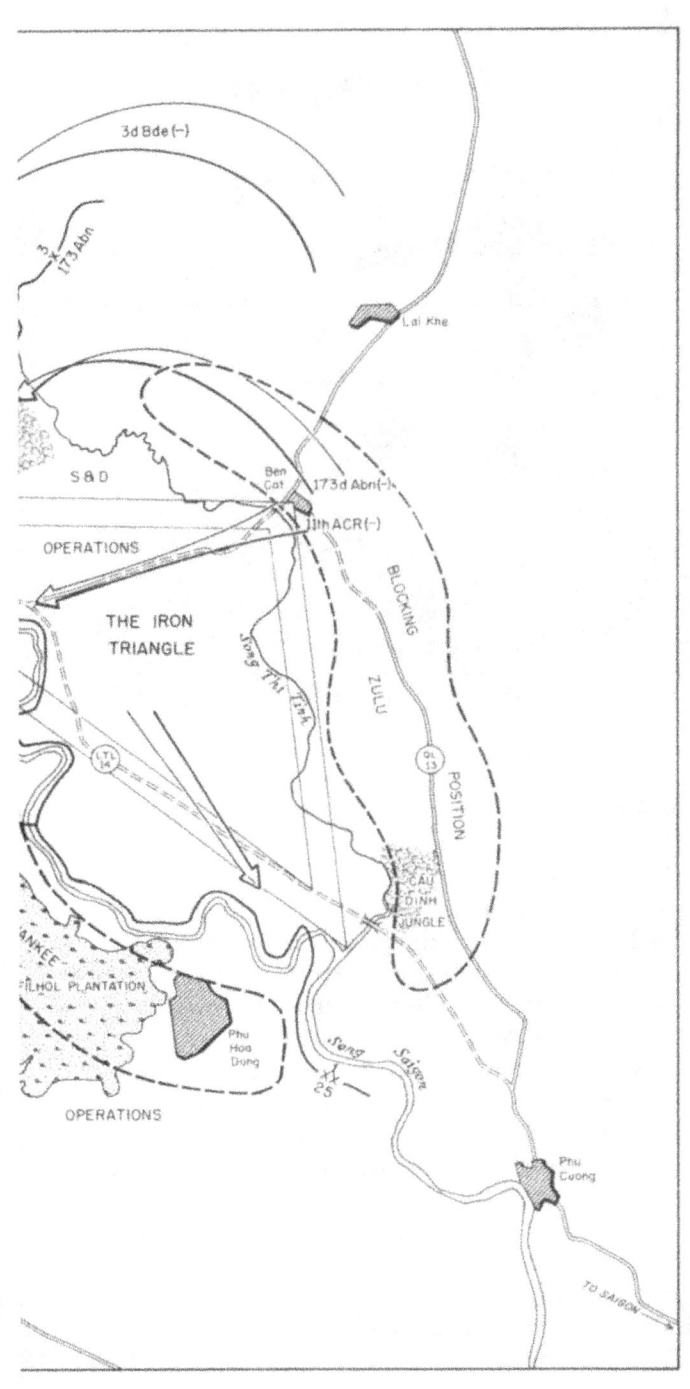

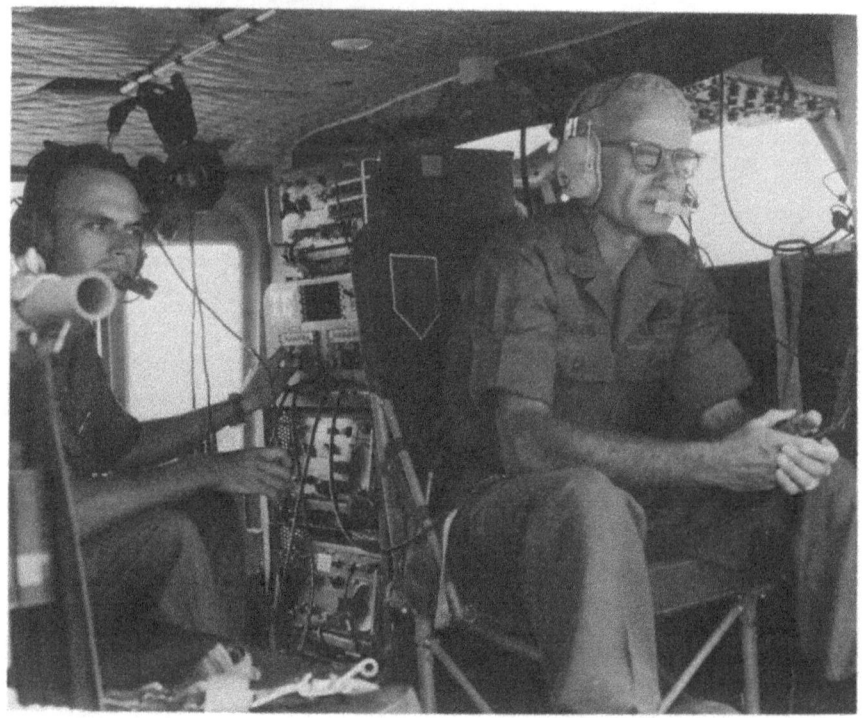

BRIGADIER GENERAL BERNARD W. ROGERS (*right*), ASSISTANT DIVISION COMMANDER OF THE 1ST INFANTRY DIVISION, *directs his troops in battle by radio, operated by First Lieutenant Christopher J. Needels. (Photograph taken in 1966.)*

contain strongly fortified positions with the routes of approach mined and booby trapped. The terrain in the area consists of dense forests and wet, open rice lands. Cover in the rice paddies, marshes, and swamps is generally limited to road embankments and dikes. Fields of fire are poor in the forests. Vehicle movement is restricted to existing roads and some trails. What few slopes exist are very gentle; the highest points in the area do not exceed forty meters.

The weather for CEDAR FALLS was most favorable during January when the northeast monsoon develops to its fullest, leaving the interior regions of the III Corps area with relatively clear skies and little precipitation. Except for periods of early morning fog and occasional morning and afternoon rain showers, cloud ceilings are unlimited and the visibility is excellent. The temperature varies from a low of 59° to a high of 95°.

The deception planned in positioning the various units was involved and critical. The 11th Armored Cavalry Regiment was to come from Xuan Loc, 100 kilometers to the east, and the 173d Airborne Brigade was operating between Ben Cat and Phuoc Vinh. Elements of the 25th Infantry Division and 196th Light Infantry Brigade were to move from the areas of Cu Chi, to the south, and Tay Ninh city, some sixty kilometers to the northwest. The 1st Infantry Division elements were to be air transported to complete the seal and invade the area. Numerous small-scale movements under the guise of local operations would position other forces.

From the first planning conference, strict security measures were enforced to prevent disclosure of the operation. The planning group was held to a minimum within II Field Force headquarters and, wherever possible, preparations were made without specifically identifying them with CEDAR FALLS. All commanders were instructed on 19 December 1966 to minimize helicopter operations during January. Even the plan for the unprecedented mass evacuation of civilians from the area was not disclosed before the operation. Planning for the transportation and housing of refugees was co-ordinated only with Mr. John Vann, director of Region III's Office of Civil Operations. Although supplies were earmarked for shipment to a refugee relocation center at Phu Cuong, no construction or stocking was started until CEDAR FALLS had commenced. General Seaman personally briefed the commanding general of the South Vietnamese III Corps on D minus 2, 6 January 1967. South Vietnamese troop participation was approved at that time with government forces assigned the missions of supporting American blocking forces, of securing and transporting civilian evacuees, and of supporting security forces in the An Loc and Quan Loi areas. The Vietnamese III Corps commander assisted in maintaining security by restricting dissemination of information on the operation.

CEDAR FALLS was to be conducted in two distinct phases. Phase I, 5-8 January, consisted of positioning units on the flanks of the Iron Triangle-Thanh Dien forest area. D-day was set for 8 January when an air assault on Ben Suc would take place. Ben Suc was to be sealed, searched, and, after evacuation of its inhabitants and their possessions, destroyed. Phase II of the operation was to start on 9 January with an armored force attacking west from the vicinity of Ben Cat to penetrate the Iron Triangle. Simultaneously, air assaults in an arc around the Thanh Dien forest from Ben Cat to Ben Suc would complete the northern portion of the encirclement of the triangle. Forces would attack south through the entire objective area to the confluence of the Saigon and Thi Tinh Rivers. All civilians were to be evacuated from the area which would be cleared and the tunnels destroyed. Phase II of Operation CEDAR FALLS was planned to last from two to three weeks.

The task organization under II Field Force consisted of three divisions: the 25th Infantry Division under the command of Major General Frederick C. Weyand; the 1st Infantry Division commanded by Major General William E. DePuy; and the South Vietnamese 5th Infantry Division, Brigadier General Phan Quoc Thuan commanding. Forces supporting the operation were the 7th Air Force; 1st Logistical Command; 3d Tactical Fighter Wing; II Field Force, Vietnam, Artillery; the 12th Combat Aviation Group; and the 79th Engineer Group. South Vietnamese supporting forces included the 3d Riverine Company (Navy), the 30th River Assault Group (Navy), and three Regional Forces boat companies.

CEDAR FALLS was to be the largest and most significant operation to this point in the war.

CHAPTER II

Positioning the Anvil—Operations Fitchburg and Niagara Falls

The U.S. 25th Division would form the anvil for CEDAR FALLS using one organic and one attached brigade positioned along the Saigon River on the southwest leg of the Iron Triangle to conduct search and destroy operations and to prevent enemy forces from escaping. Other elements of the 25th were not directly involved in the operation. The U.S. 1st Infantry Division, employing two organic brigades and one attached brigade, had a threefold mission. Before D-day the division would position elements along the Thi Tinh River, conduct search and destroy operations, and assume screening and blocking positions to keep the enemy from escaping to the east. Commencing D-day (8 January), one brigade would seal, search, clear, and destroy the village of Ben Suc. The third task would be to swing the hammer element of this hammer and anvil operation; that is, to attack west and south with one brigade through the triangle and with another through the Thanh Dien forest. One organic brigade of the division would not be employed in CEDAR FALLS.

On 5 January (D—3), the two U.S. divisions began the deception deployment of the elements which were to participate in CEDAR FALLS.

25th Infantry Division

For Operation CEDAR FALLS, the 25th Division employed its 2d Brigade and the 196th Light Infantry Brigade. Elements of the South Vietnamese 7th Regiment, 5th Infantry Division, were also placed under the control of the division.

The area of operations of the 25th extended on a line generally parallel to the Saigon River from the southern portion of the Boi Loi woods southeast to a north–south line four kilometers east of Phu Hoa Dong. This area was some twenty-five kilometers long and was designated Blocking Position YANKEE. The division's area of operation encompassed former Viet Cong havens in both the Boi Loi and Ho Bo woods and in the Filhol Plantation. The 25th Divi-

Two Armored Personnel Carriers of Company C, 1st Battalion, 5th Infantry (Mechanized), *move through the scrub jungle in search of the enemy.*

sion was also responsible for traffic control on the Saigon River. At night, ambushes were to be emplaced along the river; by day, patrols would secure the river, thereby releasing the majority of forces for search and destroy operations.

The 196th Light Infantry Brigade, commanded by Brigadier General Richard T. Knowles, was deployed from Tay Ninh to the Ho Bo woods. Under the guise of a continuation of Operation Fitchburg—an action initiated earlier in the Tay Ninh area—the 196th was to locate and destroy key enemy installations and fortifications, deny the use of the area as a logistical base and headquarters, and establish blocking positions to prevent enemy escape across the Saigon River. The operational area of the 196th comprised the northern portion of the 25th Division zone of responsibility and was fifteen kilometers long, extending parallel to the Saigon River from the Boi Loi woods on the north to the Rach (stream) Son, immediately northwest of the Filhol Plantation. The task organization included two infantry battalions, two mechanized infantry battalions, two cavalry troops, the 175th Engineer Company, and a battalion (+) of artillery.

At 0540 on D minus 3 (5 January 1967) the 196th Brigade began the move to its CEDAR FALLS operational area, using both ground and airlift. Only relatively light enemy contact was made by the 196th during this final phase of FITCHBURG. As planned, the movement placed the brigade forces in initial positions from which the northern portion of the 25th Division's area of operation could be controlled. Half of the anvil was now in place.

As the 196th maneuvered into position, the 2d Brigade, 25th Division, commanded by Colonel Marvin D. "Red" Fuller, was preparing to be committed. The brigade task organization included two infantry battalions, one tank battalion, two artillery battalions (one each in direct and general support), and an engineer company. Other brigade units included one troop of cavalry (attached on D-day) and a military intelligence detachment.

The 2d Brigade area of responsibility was parallel to and west of the Saigon River from a north–south line four kilometers east of Phu Hoa Dong to the northern perimeter of the Filhol Plantation. The brigade's mission was to block along the Saigon River "early on D plus 1" (9 January) and prevent enemy escape from the Iron Triangle area. Other tasks included maintaining control over the river, preventing its use by enemy forces, and destroying enemy forces and installations in the area of operation, to include the elimination of the hostile infrastructure in the village of Phu Hoa Dong. This last requirement was to be accomplished in conjunction with a South Vietnamese battalion as a "Buddy" operation and was designed to expand government control over the village. Phu Hoa Dong, a complex of hamlets including Ben Co, Phu Loi, and Phu Thuan, located to the west of the Filhol Plantation, was a known enemy communications and liaison point. It was from Phu Hoa Dong that commercial products and taxes could be procured by the Viet Cong 2d Battalion, 165th Regiment, a unit which occupied areas to the east of the town.

Movement by the 2d Brigade into the blocking positions to complete the anvil would begin at 0400 on D-day.

1st Infantry Division

The 1st Infantry Division was to be employed both to block on the east and to conduct extensive search and destroy, tunnel and base camp destruction, and jungle clearing operations throughout the area. In addition, 1st Division forces would constitute the hammer of the operation. Like the 25th, the 1st Division initiated

BRIGADIER GENERAL JOHN R. DEANE, JR., COMMANDING GENERAL OF THE 173D AIRBORNE BRIGADE, *checks the location of a patrol.*

preparatory action for CEDAR FALLS on 5 January, D minus 3, in a cover operation dubbed NIAGARA FALLS. Major forces included the division's 2d and 3d Brigades plus the 173d Airborne Brigade and the 11th Armored Cavalry Regiment (minus one squadron) placed under operational control of the division. For this operation the 173d was code-named Task Force DEANE, for its commander, Brigadier General John R. Deane, Jr.

NIAGARA FALLS was a three-day operation assigned to Task Force DEANE; it began at 0730 on 5 January. Similar to Operation FITCHBURG conducted by the 196th Light Infantry Brigade, NIAGARA FALLS was a deception designed to place combat elements in position before striking the main blow. The area of operation included the terrain between the Thi Tinh River and Highway 13, bounded on the north by the Cau Dinh jungle and extending south approximately four kilometers. This terrain lies immediately east of the southern point of the Iron Triangle. It was believed that the 2d and 3d Battalions of the 165th Viet Cong Main Force Regiment, the

Phu Loi Battalion, and a Viet Cong company (the 63d) might be operating in the area.

NIAGARA FALLS terminated at 1500 on 7 January without major incident. As with the 25th Division units, a deceptive move had resulted in tactical units being positioned, in this case, in Blocking Position ZULU. Enemy escape routes to the east were now closed. Elements of Task Force DEANE would form part of the hammer forces swinging west through the triangle on D plus 1.

Among the accomplishments of NIAGARA FALLS, perhaps the most noteworthy was that of the 1st Engineers. Working with a task force of fifty bulldozers, Lieutenant Colonel Joseph M. Kiernan, Jr.'s troops cleared 365 acres of dense jungle containing many Viet Cong installations and serving as an access route to the Iron Triangle.

The 2d Brigade of the 1st Infantry Division was to seal and search the village of Ben Suc, prepare to evacuate the inhabitants and their possessions, and eliminate the village as a center of Viet Cong operations. The tactical command post along with one infantry battalion left Di An early on 7 January for a road march to the airfield at Bien Hoa. From there the units were airlifted to Dau Tieng. Also on the 7th, the 1st Battalion, 26th Infantry, the unit designated to make the actual assault on Ben Suc, was air transported from Phuoc Vinh to Dau Tieng and came under the operational control of the 2d Brigade. As D-day approached, elements of the 2d Brigade waited in readiness, and the tension mounted.

The third major element of the 1st Division, the 3d Brigade, was slated for search and destroy operations around and through the Thanh Dien forest as a part of the hammer. The operations order was issued to participating battalions of the brigade on 5 January, and the subsequent days were used for planning and preparation. On 8 January the brigade's direct support battalion moved from Lai Khe to Artillery Base I, two kilometers from Ben Cat at the northeast corner of the Iron Triangle. The 3d Brigade was almost ready for its H-hour on D plus 1—0800, 9 January 1967.

The "Blue Spaders" of the 1st Battalion, 26th Infantry, were set for their raid on Ben Suc; the anvil was ready for emplacement and the hammer was poised. CEDAR FALLS time had arrived.

CHAPTER III

D-Day—Ben Suc

The II Field Force, Vietnam, tactical command post for Operation CEDAR FALLS opened at 0700 on D-day at Long Binh. Under its direction the twenty battalions allocated to the five brigades of the 1st and 25th Infantry Divisions were ready for Phase II of CEDAR FALLS—the destruction of the enemy force.

25th Infantry Division

Elements of the 25th Infantry Division's 2d Brigade started its participation in CEDAR FALLS early on 8 January 1967. By 0730 the first contingent of troops had been airlifted to a forward base within five hundred meters of the Saigon River, near its junction with the Thi Tinh, and two kilometers east of Phu Hoa Dong. Enemy resistance was encountered on the second lift and, despite repeated air strikes and artillery barrages, contact continued throughout the afternoon; however, friendly casualties were light. The enemy withdrew under cover of darkness. Two companies of the 2d Brigade now anchored the southeastern flank of the 25th Division. Later *Chieu Hoi* returnees reported the assault had confronted the battalion headquarters and a company of a battalion of the 165th Regiment, and some sixty Viet Cong had been killed and fifty-five wounded. Documents captured in the area confirmed the presence of this battalion; according to the 2d Brigade's report, "this was the only incident during the entire operation in which the Viet Cong elected to fight." To the northwest of this action, the brigade's other two battalions attacked northeast from Cu Chi through the Filhol Plantation and by nightfall were in position at the edge of the plantation, four to five hundred meters south of the Saigon River.

To the northwest of the 2d Brigade's positions, the 196th Brigade continued its search of the Ho Bo woods, uncovering a small quantity of enemy supplies.

The anvil was in position.

1st Infantry Division

To the east, General Deane's task force remained in blocking positions along the eastern leg of the Iron Triangle. All that remained was to position the hammer forces, the 173d Brigade (Task Force DEANE) and the 3d Brigade of the "Big Red One."

Task Force DEANE officially joined Operation CEDAR FALLS at 0800 on D-day with its headquarters located near Ben Cat. Two of its battalions were lifted by helicopter from Bien Hoa to Phu Loi and then to Position BLUE, a staging area ten kilometers east of the triangle. On D-day the 11th Armored Cavalry (Blackhorse) Regiment, commanded by Colonel William W. Cobb, came under the operational control of the 1st Division and subsequently under Task Force DEANE at 1200. The cavalry had closed its trains and headquarters in a staging area north of Phu Loi at about midnight the previous day. The 3d Squadron of the 11th had moved from its base camp at Long Giao to a forward assembly area just east of the junction of the Saigon and Thi Tinh Rivers, the last element arriving at 2315 on D minus 1.

The 3d Brigade (the "Iron" Brigade), commanded by Colonel Sidney M. ("Mickey") Marks, moved its forces to staging areas at Lai Khe and Dau Tieng without incident. The hammer was raised awaiting the next day, D plus 1.

Meanwhile, to the northwest of the Ho Bo woods the 1st Division's 2d Brigade under the command of Colonel James A. "Alex" Grimsley had launched the 1st Battalion, 26th Infantry (commanded by Lieutenant Colonel Alexander M. Haig), by air assault into the village of Ben Suc. (*Map 7*)

Ben Suc Village

Ensuring the dominance of the Viet Cong in the Iron Triangle area was the village of Ben Suc, located in a loop of the Saigon River at the far northwest corner of the triangle. It was an enemy-controlled village, a fortified supply and political center, and the hub of an area estimated to contain approximately six thousand persons. The village had been under firm enemy control since at least 1964 when a South Vietnamese battalion was driven out by the enemy. Before that, the government's influence had been tenuous at best. The central organization for the Viet Cong's Long Nguyen secret base was located in and operated from Ben Suc. The people of the village were organized into four rear service companies. One company moved rice and other supplies in sampans on the Saigon

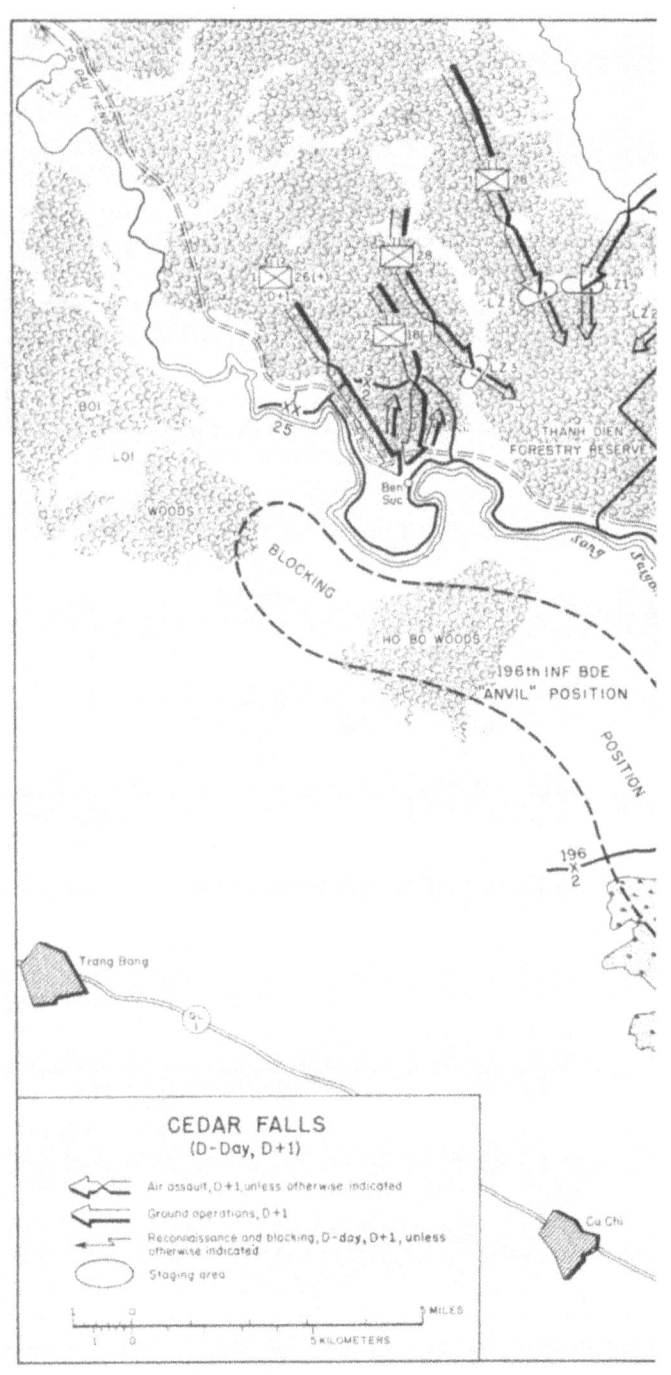

MAP 7

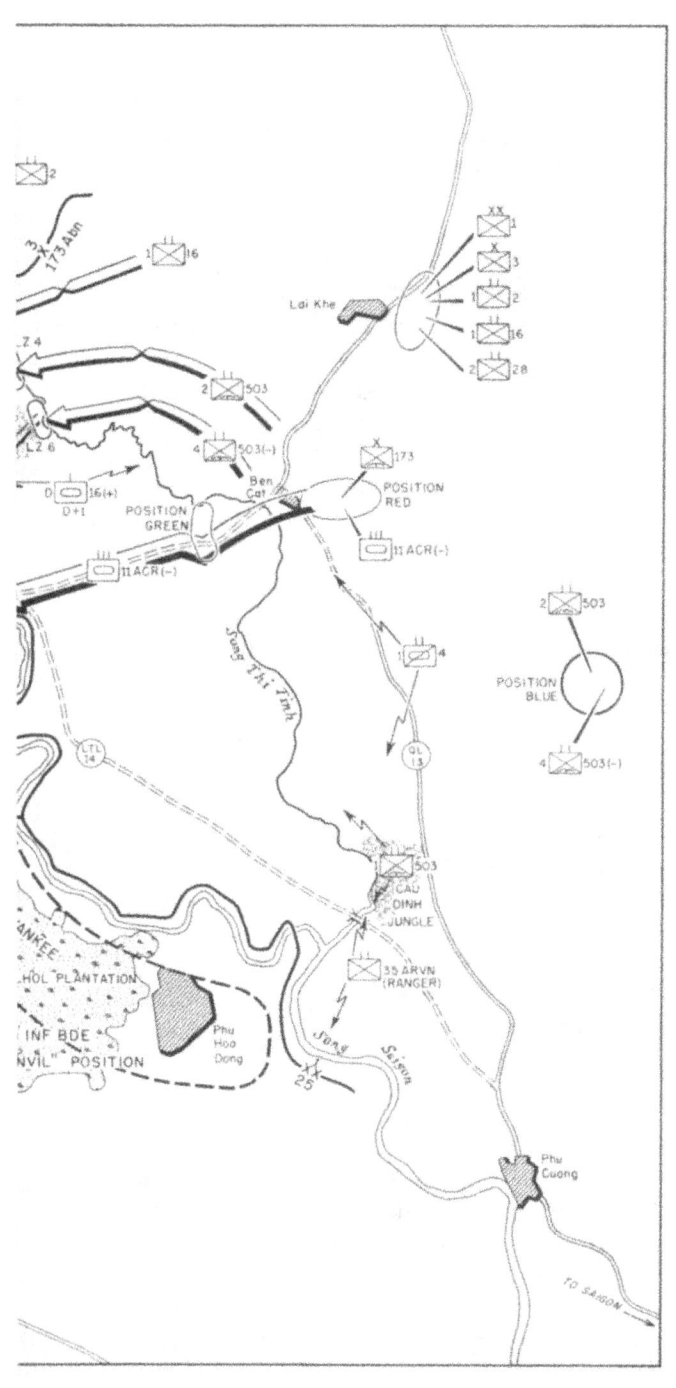

River. A second company unloaded these supplies. The two remaining companies stored the materiel in and around the village or in the nearby jungle. Just as the Iron Triangle was the key to Viet Cong influence in Saigon–Gia Dinh, so was Ben Suc the key to Viet Cong control of the Iron Triangle. This fact was well known to the province chief of Binh Duong, who for some months had been urging a military operation against the village.

Because of its importance to the enemy, Ben Suc had been marked for attention at the outset of Operation CEDAR FALLS. It was necessary to take this village and deny the enemy its future use; it was to be totally evacuated and destroyed. All inhabitants and their possessions—livestock, food, furnishings—were to be moved as humanely as possible to a government-operated relocation camp at Phu Cuong and ultimately resettled in another area. It was estimated that nearly 3,500 persons lived in Ben Suc and another 2,500 in the vicinity, most of whom lived in the three villages of Rach Kien, Bung Cong, and Rach Bap along the northern edge of the triangle. These villages were also to be evacuated.

The perimeter of Ben Suc was expected to be heavily mined and booby trapped. Viet Cong units reported in the area included the 7th Battalion, 165th Viet Cong Regiment, and the 61st Local Force Company.

This attack had to be a swift, decisive strike directly into the enemy stronghold, not the methodical probing technique used in previous operations. A plan for a massive assault by helicopter into the village itself was visualized—over four hundred men and sixty helicopters simultaneously—total surprise! There would be no preparatory fires. The air assault, placing one reinforced infantry battalion inside the village within a minimum time, would quickly seal the village. Further landings would bring in support troops and artillery as well as troops to initiate search and interrogation; the orderly evacuation of the inhabitants would follow, and, finally, the village would be destroyed.

The Initial Assault

The sight of sixty helicopters flying in formation and zooming into Ben Suc at treetop level was one which none who witnessed will ever forget. Here is the way it was described by Staff Sergeant Frank P. Castro, writing in the 28 January 1967 issue of the 1st Division paper, *The American Traveler:*

In the early morning hours, January 8, people in Ben Suc Village went calmly about their tasks. At exactly 8 a.m., total confusion erupted. The once-clear sky filled with 60 helicopters. The choppers swooped in, allowing division soldiers to unload and begin a seal of the village. Minutes later the sky was filled again as the aircraft vanished as quickly as they had appeared.

Planning of this dramatic air mission was assigned to the 1st Aviation Battalion on 5 January. Major Nick J. Primis was the battalion operations officer. He explained: "We were faced with a multitude of problems. We had to lift an entire infantry battalion in addition to an attached company from Dau Tieng to Ben Suc and we were supposed to put the battalion on the ground at exactly 8 a.m. Further, the element of surprise was in our hands. Nothing—artillery, airstrikes or gunships—was to hit the area until after we had put the troops on the ground. This was the first time that we were going to land in a town."

The aviation battalion commander, Lieutenant Colonel Algin S. Hawkins and his staff prepared maps, photo mosaics, operations orders, and photo obliques, picked routes in and out of the village, and timed the mission to the second.

Each flight leader had clear, detailed pictures of his landing zone thanks to Major Cecil O. Carlile, the Aerial Surveillance and Target Acquisition Platoon commander, who flew a Mohawk airplane over Ben Suc, photographing the entire area from 6,000 feet.

At 6:00 A.M. in pitch darkness, sixty "slicks" (troop carriers) and ten gun ships began arriving at the Dau Tieng airstrip. Sergeant Alton B. Pinkney was a pathfinder with the 1st Aviation Battalion. His jobs included the marking of landing zones, directing aircraft to and from loading areas, and supervising loading. On January 8th he stood on the airstrip armed with a large flashlight and two batonlike lights; twenty aircraft hovered overhead awaiting his guidance to land. When the ships were finally loaded, Pinkney recalled, "They lifted off beautifully, but once they were airborne I wondered: How in the hell are they going to get those ships lined up?"

By 7:25 the flight was orbiting Dau Tieng. The helicopters slipped over, under, and around each other as pilots jockeyed their craft into position less than fifty feet from the chopper in front. They had twenty minutes to form into two "V" formations, with three flights of ten choppers in each.

The nineteen-mile route plotted by Colonel Hawkins ran almost due south from Dau Tieng over the dense Boi Loi jungle and then curved sharply to the east. So well timed was the trip that at one point the aviators passed a control point just fifteen seconds ahead of schedule; a slight change in heading put them back on time. At a road junction near Suoi Cau (the third control point in the route), the ships turned east and dropped to treetop level. They skimmed along at about eighty-five miles an hour, heading toward another control point and Ben Suc.

At the highway release point, the pilots spotted smoke tossed by pathfinders, cut left, hopped over the Cachua Forestry Reserve (at the southeastern tip of the Boi Loi Woods) at over 100 miles an hour and swarmed into Ben Suc.

Flying a gunship, Major George B. Fish, from the 1st Aviation Battalion, zoomed over the trees to mark three key landing zones while the main flight was one minute out.

His crew chief recalled, "We were flying in one area when I heard over the radio 'Rebel 36, go in for the mark.' We went in at low level at about

Private First Class Willie Foxworth, Company A, 1st Battalion, 28th Infantry, *takes a position behind weathered graves.*

eighty-five miles an hour. We received fire from a bunker and returned it. . . . It didn't fire anymore. . . . And you look out to see a whole bunch of choppers . . . you see a fantastic mess . . . beautifully coordinated and planned."

Major Robert E. Oberg, Commanding Officer of D Troop, 1st Squadron, 4th Cavalry, and Captain William B. Owens were orbiting south of the Cachua Reserve leading "choppers" loaded with light infantry fire teams—"Eagle Flights." They followed the troop carriers into Ben Suc and blocked to the south, ultimately accounting for five enemy killed, two prisoners, and thirty sampans destroyed.

Major Donald A. Ice, the commander of A Company, led his flight over the jungle and along the river to a landing zone in the northeast corner of Ben Suc. "As we flew along the river our skids were almost in the water," he recalled. "Then we jumped a treeline, flared up and popped into the landing zone. I had to push Vietnamese out of the zone. They didn't know what was happening."

The choppers touched down simultaneously in landing zones to the west, north, and east of the town while the "Eagle Flight" guarded the south. In less than one and one-half minutes an entire infantry battalion, some 420 men, was on the ground.

Some small arms fire was received but was quickly suppressed. The troops occupied blocking positions primarily to prevent movement out of the village. At 0805, preplanned artillery and air strikes were directed into the woods north of the village to discourage the use of those escape routes. At 0830 more troops were landed to the south of the village as a blocking force on that potential escape route. The village was sealed.

Just after the assault ships had departed, helicopters with loudspeakers and South Vietnamese Army announcers aboard circled the village at low altitude and broadcast the following message:

> Attention people of Ben Suc. You are surrounded by Republic of South Vietnam and allied forces. Do not run away or you will be shot as VC. Stay in your homes and wait for further instructions.

The inhabitants were then further instructed to go immediately to the old schoolhouse.

Most of the villagers followed the instructions; those who attempted to evade and leave the village were engaged by the blocking forces. Adjacent rivers were patrolled for any escapees. Tactical surprise was almost complete; the enemy was unable to offer any cohesive resistance to the landing.

By 1030, 8 January, Ben Suc was securely in the hands of the friendly forces and the 2d Brigade command post had been established in the village. During the two and one-half hours since the initial landing, a total of forty enemy had been killed in action, with only light friendly casualties.

Company A, 1st Battalion, 26th Infantry, was one of the first units on the ground and quickly formed up after clearing its landing zone. As the point squad moved forward from the landing zone toward its designated blocking position, tragedy struck. Two command-detonated claymore mines exploded and two men fell. A large booby trap mounted in a tree exploded and its fragments downed two more men. The squad had wandered into an enemy minefield. Staff Sergeant Ernest Williams of San Francisco, California, rushed forward to set up security for the wounded and to get them medical aid. The platoon medical corpsman was injured when he stepped on an antipersonnel mine while trying to aid the wounded. Specialist Four Astor Rogers of Chicago, Illinois, another medic, hurried forward. When enemy sniper fire began coming in on his position, Sergeant Williams brought his men on line and laid down a base of fire in co-ordination with his platoon leader. "Through enemy fire and a heavy mine field these men functioned with total disregard for their own lives and safety," said

Captain Rudolf Egersdorfer, Company A commander. "They are a credit to the unit."

After the village was sealed and the troops had consolidated their positions, a South Vietnamese battalion was airlanded into Ben Suc to search the village and interrogate the villagers. (It was no coincidence that the South Vietnamese battalion selected was the same one which had been driven out of Ben Suc in 1964.) The search uncovered a number of tunnel and bunker complexes in which the South Vietnamese forces engaged the enemy sporadically for some three days and nights. In the destruction of these facilities, the South Vietnamese forces were assisted by the division chemical section tunnel team, attached to the 1st Battalion, 26th Infantry. The team was successful in using a new technique in tunnel destruction. After demolition charges had been strung throughout the tunnel system, the entrances were sealed and acetylene was pumped in and ignited throughout the system by the charges; this process rendered the tunnel useless and destroyed anything left inside.

As the methodical search by South Vietnamese forces continued, under some houses were discovered as many as three levels of carefully concealed storage rooms. Great stores of rice of high quality were found. Just outside the village, searchers turned up a large cache of enemy medical supplies, including surgical instruments and 800,000 vials of penicillin. Of the more than 7,500 enemy uniforms found during CEDAR FALLS, many were uncovered at Ben Suc.

The civilians were interrogated and classified into appropriate categories. Interrogation was conducted by the 1st Republic of Vietnam Military Intelligence Detachment and members of the S-2 section of the 2d Brigade, 1st U.S. Infantry Division. All males between the ages of 15 and 45 were segregated for further questioning while other villagers were instructed and assisted in their preparations for evacuation. Since the inhabitants of Ben Suc had not received medical assistance for three years and were in only fair health, South Vietnamese and U.S. medical teams examined them and provided medical and dental care as they awaited interrogation.

Following the interrogations and screening, 106 individuals were detained; of these, 28 were classified as Viet Cong. Most of them were local Viet Cong who had virtually no information and were of little intelligence value. However, a Viet Cong platoon leader of Group 83—the major unit in the area—was captured. His platoon transported rice in the general area around Ben Suc. Among the well-dressed individuals picked up at Ben Suc were some high-ranking political and propaganda cadres from Hanoi. Included in the group was a mathematics professor educated at Peking University who was caught trying to escape through the rice paddies on the south of the village.

Although the responsibility for evacuating the inhabitants of Ben Suc and the villages on the northern edge of the triangle fell to the South Vietnamese, assistance on the U.S. side came under the control of Major Robert L. Schweitzer, commander of the 1st Division Revolutionary Development task force. (Major Schweitzer was familiarly referred to by his radio call sign, "Helper 6.") It was to be expected that uprooting the natives of these villages would evoke resentment, and it did. They had lived under and with the Viet Cong and had supported them for the past three years; nor was it easy for the natives to give up their homes and the land they had been working. The villagers were permitted to take with them anything they could carry, pull, or herd, to include their water buffalo. What they could not take was retrieved by the U.S. and South Vietnamese troops and returned to the natives at the relocation center. A total of 5,987 persons was evacuated (582 men, 1,651 women, and 3,754 children). Also moved to the relocation site were 247 water buffalo, 225 head of cattle, 158 oxcarts, and 60 tons of rice.

When the evacuation commenced there was no usable road into Ben Suc. Even though the engineers set about repairing the road from Rach Bap to Ben Suc over which supplies and evacuees were later moved, initially evacuation was by South Vietnamese Navy boats and U.S. Chinook helicopters. As pathetic and pitiful as was the sight of the natives of Ben Suc with their carts, chickens, hogs, rice, and all else waiting to be transported to the temporary camp at Phu Cuong, there were still moments of humor, even for the evacuees. For example, a handful of soldiers tried unsuccessfully to get a huge—and dangerous—water buffalo loaded onto a boat, only to be embarrassed when the 11-year-old buffalo driver appeared and talked his animal on board. There was even one occasion when a search was made throughout the relocation camp for a particular buffalo driver whose assistance was needed back at the loading site at Ben Suc.

At one point in the evacuation, a sow became separated from her twelve pigs as they were being loaded on one of the giant Chinook helicopters. She loudly made her loss known. General DePuy, who happened to stop by the loading site and learned of the mishap, instructed: "I want that sow reunited with her pigs before nightfall." Before long, Helper 6 had the sow on her way to the relocation camp.

Many difficulties were faced during the evacuation of the populace. However, they were relatively few and small in comparison with those problems facing the members of the U.S. Office of Civil Operations who were charged with assisting the South Vietnamese in preparing and operating the relocation center. As General Westmoreland has stated: "Unfortunately, the resettlement phase was not as well planned or executed as the actual evacuation. For the first several days the families suffered unnecessary hardships." Part of the problem resulted from the security measures taken during the planning phase. Thanks to the immediate assistance of a task force from the Big Red One under Major Carl R. Grantham, latrines were dug, wood and water were made available, a buffalo wallow was dug and filled with water, a cattle enclosure was built, dozens of Arctic tents were pitched, and hardships were eased for the displaced families.

On 10 January 1967, the South Vietnamese 1st Airborne Task Force of two battalions arrived at Ben Suc with the mission of relieving the U.S. battalion of its responsibilities in sealing the village. Further, the task force was to assist in securing and screening the populace of Ben Suc and nearby villages. At this time the South Vietnamese battalion already at Ben Suc was attached to the airborne task force. With the continuing, systematic evacuation of Ben Suc under the control of South Vietnamese forces, and with the village seal taken over by the South Vietnamese task force, U.S. 1st Division troops were freed for deployment into other areas of the CEDAR FALLS operation. All that remained for 1st Division troops was the razing of Ben Suc after its inhabitants had been removed.

As the villagers and their belongings moved out, bulldozers, tankdozers, and demolition teams moved in. Since Ben Suc was not yet totally deserted, the initial dozers set about clearing a scrub jungle area in the southwest corner of the village known by the troops as the briar patch. As Colonel Kiernan, commanding officer of the 1st Engineer Battalion, recalled:

. . . I guess it was about twenty acres of scrub jungle. . . . The place was so infested with tunnels that as my dozers would knock over the stumps of trees, the VC would pop out from behind the dozers. We captured about . . . six or eight VC one morning. They just popped out of the tunnels and we picked them up. . . . After the civilians were taken from the town, we went through and methodically knocked down the homes . . . tunnels were throughout the whole area. . . .

The bulldozers moved through the former Viet Cong stronghold and razed the structures to the ground, crushing ruins, collapsing tunnels, and obliterating bunkers and underground storage rooms. When the village had been flattened by the engineers, there was yet one more blow to be dealt to Ben Suc by Colonel Kiernan's professionals. A large cavity was scooped out near the center of the area, filled with ten thousand pounds of explosives—many no longer usable in normal operations, covered, tamped, and then set off by a chemical fuze within minutes of the predicted time of detonation. The hope was that the blast might crush any undiscovered tunnels in the village.

One of the major objectives of Operation CEDAR FALLS had been achieved; the village of Ben Suc no longer existed. What about the hammer operation—had it swung and with what effect?

CHAPTER IV

Phase II—The Hammer Swings

As dawn broke on D plus 1 (9 January 1967) the units forming the anvil of CEDAR FALLS were maneuvering into their final positions as the 1st Division's 2d Brigade continued its day-old operation in Ben Suc. The hammer forces of the 1st Infantry Division (the organic 3d Brigade and Task Force DEANE) initiated their assault at 0800 with simultaneous attacks across the Iron Triangle and into the Thanh Dien forest. The impact of the hammer on enemy forces was imminent.

3d Brigade

The mission of the Iron Brigade was to conduct airmobile assaults with five battalions into the Thanh Dien forest, conduct search and destroy operations to kill or capture enemy forces, destroy enemy installations, and evacuate all inhabitants from the area of operations. The operations order had been issued to all participating battalions on 5 January, and the previous four days had been spent in detailed planning and preparation. The initial positions for the elements of the 3d Brigade formed a semicircle to the north of the Thanh Dien forest. Six landing zones (LZ's) were designated. The terrain in this area ranges from flat to gently rolling; the undergrowth is dense. The few streams in the area are fordable with minor difficulty.

The 3d Brigade's area of operation, according to intelligence sources, was thought to be an important supply base and hospital area. The enemy units believed to be in the area were listed as base caretaker elements and headquarters defense units. The Americans expected to find base camps and supply installations and well-constructed bunkers, tunnels, and trenches, all protected by extensive mines and booby traps. These expectations proved to be accurate.

Major units constituting the task organization of the 3d Brigade included five infantry battalions, two cavalry squadrons, and one artillery battalion.

At 0735, 9 January, an extensive air and artillery preparation began on Landing Zone 1, the northernmost point of the ring of men and weapons that was soon to be formed around the Thanh

First Sergeant George L. Taylor, Company C., 2d Battalion, 28th Infantry, *inspects captured enemy mortar rounds.*

Dien forest. For the 3d Brigade and the 1st Battalion, 2d Infantry, commanded by Lieutenant Colonel William C. Simpson, Operation CEDAR FALLS began at 0800 as the first of sixty helicopters touched down. The entire battalion was on the ground in less than five minutes. The artillery and air strikes turned three kilometers toward the east and Landing Zone 2. At 0840 Lieutenant Colonel Rufus C. Lazzell and the 1st Battalion, 16th Infantry, joined the battle. At 0910 the first enemy reaction to this portion of the operation occurred in the vincinity of Landing Zone 1 in the form of small arms fire. There were no casualties. By this time the preparatory fires had shifted to the west and Landing Zone 3.

The 2d Battalion, 28th Infantry, under the command of Lieutenant Colonel Elmer D. Pendleton, started landing at LZ 3 at 0920. As the battalion expanded its zone of operations, the first indications that the enemy was retreating were noted. Within twenty minutes the infantrymen had found several freshly dug foxholes, recent oxcart tracks, a tunnel containing a pot of steaming rice, and a cache of munitions. Located next was a 55-gallon drum of diesel fuel, a 66-pound enemy mine, and a newly constructed base camp. Two light observation helicopters overflying the area of operation were hit by ground fire and so damaged that they had to be evacuated. Small quantities of weapons and munitions continued to be found.

At 1155 the 1st Battalion, 28th Infantry, commanded by Lieutenant Colonel Jack G. Whitted, touched down on Landing Zone 5, located between Landing Zones 1 and 3, and began search and destroy operations.

By noon the 2d Battalion, 28th Infantry, was reporting sniper fire and seeing an unknown number of Viet Cong escaping to the south on bicycles. Near Landing Zone 3 the battalion found an arms cache in an enemy base camp which included 2 recoilless rifles, 1 60-mm. mortar, and 135 Russian rifles. In the same area they soon uncovered some grenades, 24 gas masks, 75 tons of rice, and 4.5 tons of salt.

By midafternoon the 3d Brigade set up a forward command post for communications at the now secured village of Ben Suc. The battalions of the brigade now in the operational area continued their search and were uncovering large quantities of materiel and abandoned enemy installations.

At 1350 the 2d Battalion, 18th Infantry (less Company A), passed to the operational control of the 3d Brigade and prepared to air assault into the operational area. At 1600, as the first lift of the battalion under the command of Lieutenant Colonel Lewis R. Baumann was going into a landing zone three kilometers south of LZ 3, two claymore mines were detonated by the enemy. An alternate landing site was designated three kilometers to the west where the battalion landed without incident. The battalion then reverted to the operational control of the 2d Brigade.

At 1820 the 2d Battalion, 28th Infantry, apprehended sixty persons four kilometers north of Landing Zone 3. They were moved to the evacuee holding area at Ben Suc.

As darkness fell, night defensive positions were established by these five combat battalions now in the Thanh Dien forest sanctuary of the Viet Cong.

Task Force Deane

At 0800 on 9 January the 11th Armored Cavalry Regiment attacked west from its staging areas near Ben Cat. After securing the bridge across the Thi Tinh River and Position GREEN, one kilometer to the southwest, the regiment knifed toward its objectives some seven kilometers to the west. By 1000 the Blackhorse

PHASE II—THE HAMMER SWINGS

MEMBERS OF THE 503D INFANTRY AND OF THE 11TH ARMORED CAVALRY *in Thanh Dien forest.*

Regiment had penetrated the entire width of the Iron Triangle from east to west and had severed it from the Thanh Dien forest on the north. Only slight enemy resistance had been encountered.

The 2d Battalion, 503d Infantry, commanded by Lieutenant Colonel Robert H. Sigholtz, air assaulted at 1115 into Landing Zone 4 on the northeast perimeter of the semicircle encompassing the Thanh Dien forest. By 1145 the battalion had linked up with the infantrymen of the 1st Division who had landed earlier.

Landing Zone 6, the eastern anchor of the tightening ring around the forest, was the next to be occupied by 1st Division forces. At 1235 the 4th Battalion of the 503d Infantry (–), commanded by Lieutenant Colonel Michael D. Healy, air assaulted into Landing Zone 6 and seventy minutes later had joined forces with the 2d Battalion. Blocking positions were established and limited search and destroy operations conducted. These two battalions of the 503d brought the total number in and around the Thanh Dien forest to seven.

Meanwhile, to the south, the 1st Battalion, 503d Infantry (Lieutenant Colonel Robert W. Brownlee), and 35th Ranger Battalion (with elements of the 1st Squadron, 4th Cavalry) maintained the blocking positions opposite the southeast side of the triangle held since the termination of NIAGARA FALLS.

25th Infantry Division

On D plus 1 the anvil forces of the 25th Infantry Division assumed, prepared, and improved their final blocking positions and actively conducted search and destroy operations along the west bank of the Saigon River. Tankdozers assisted in clearing the areas.

Units of the 2d Brigade continued operations in the southern sector of the division area of responsibility. At 1645 at a point on the Saigon River four kilometers northwest of Phu Hoa Dong, Company B, 2d Battalion, 34th Armor, engaged a raft with fifteen Viet Cong aboard. Employing 90-mm. guns loaded with "cannister and shot," the men of Company B destroyed the raft and killed all occupants. The brigade continued to find quantities of munitions, weapons, and rice in the numerous huts, tunnels, and bunkers, many of which were mined and booby trapped. Three sampans were located and destroyed.

The 196th Light Infantry Brigade continued its mission in the northern area of the division sector. The hamlet of A Go Noi (1) was searched and the inhabitants screened; a medical team, part of the search and destroy forces, treated the inhabitants. Nine Viet Cong were shot as they tried to cross the river during the hours of darkness. Several classified papers were captured during the day, documents which pertained to the postal, communications, and transportation section of Military Region IV. One paper classified top secret concerned economy of ammunition by Viet Cong units. It stated that ammunition could no longer be provided for American weapons and that in the future money would be furnished for the purchase of such ammunition. It went on to say that ammunition for Chinese weapons would be limited. The paper included a price list for weapons and ammunition that the Viet Cong should use when making purchases.

Small Unit Actions

Operation CEDAR FALLS was characterized by small unit actions. Typical are those of Company C, 2d Battalion, 503d Infantry, on 9 January as reported in the 173d Brigade's after action report.

On the morning of 9 January Company C was located in Position BLUE, ten kilometers east of the Iron Triangle. At 1055 the company was airlifted out of its pickup zone and twenty minutes later landed in LZ 4 on the northeast corner of the perimeter surrounding the Thanh Dien forest. Its mission was patrolling, forming blocking positions, and setting up night ambushes.

Each rifleman of the company was armed with an M16 rifle, 400 rounds of ammunition, 2 smoke grenades, and 2 fragmentary grenades. There were 2 M60 machine guns in each of the three platoons; each gunner carried a total of 1,500 rounds of ammunition. In addition, each squad had 2 M79's (grenade launchers) with 45 rounds per grenadier and an average of 2 claymore mines. The company as a whole was equipped with 3 81-mm. mortars with 30 rounds per mortar. Each individual carried 3 C-ration meals while on operations.

By 1130 on 9 January the company had cleared its landing zone and was establishing a blocking position. Captain Thomas P. Carney, the company commander, moved to the right flank to co-ordinate with the commander of the unit to the north—Company B, 1st Battalion, 16th Infantry. With the co-ordination completed, the company's three platoons established defensive positions along an oxcart trail west of the Thi Tinh River. The company's area of operation was primarily dense jungle with the exception of one section which had been defoliated within the last year. Based upon an assessment of the situation and terrain by the two adjacent company commanders, night ambush patrols were to be placed on an overgrown trail in the western portion of the perimeter.

After the defensive position had been established, patrols were sent out to search the immediate area for signs of the enemy and for possible ambush sites. The 3d Platoon soon discovered a hut connected to a combination tunnel and bomb shelter. That the hut had been inhabited recently was confirmed by the freshly cooked rice which was found. Further search of the area revealed a cache of twelve bicycles and 200 pounds of polished rice on a concrete platform. Everything was destroyed with the exception of the bicycles, which were later to provide transportation for the men of "Charlie" Company while in base camp.

The 33-man weapons platoon found one small hut while screening to the rear of the company command post. After destroying the hut, the platoon moved east toward the Thi Tinh River and found a fordable stream. The platoon then returned to the company base area.

Sergeant Nathaniel King was in charge of the 1st Platoon's patrol. Two foxholes were discovered; neither showed signs of recent use. Sergeant King also reported finding a footpath running parallel to the overgrown trail in the western portion of the company's position. Although the trail showed no signs of recent use, there was evidence that the small footpath was heavily traveled, probably because it could not be observed from the air.

All patrols returned to the command post by 1630. Hot A-rations and a .50-caliber machine gun arrived by resupply choppers, and the company settled down to warm chow.

During darkness the company employed three-man listening posts around its position. One post located between the 2d and 3d Platoon positions was occupied by Sergeant Frank Bothwell, Specialist Four Walter Johnson, and Private First Class Joseph Russo. They had moved into position shortly after nightfall, situating themselves three meters from one another in a triangular position for easy communication and 360-degree observation. The terrain was generally flat and overgrown with elephant grass and bamboo. The men were instructed not to engage the enemy unless absolutely necessary.

The three men lay quietly. After minutes of silence, movement was detected at about 1940 at a distance of approximately fifty meters. The noise became louder. Because of the thick vegetation, vision was limited. The men were prone and could not move without being detected. The enemy was now nearly on top of the position. Sergeant Bothwell knew that if he reached for his M16, the noise would be heard; he prepared to throw a fragmentation grenade instead.

Johnson was in a better position to observe the enemy; however, he knew he must come to a sitting position to fire and would thereby expose himself and his comrades. However, as the enemy came closer, Johnson realized that the time for action had come. He sprang to a sitting position and fired approximately five rounds before his weapon jammed. An enemy grenade exploded and a fragment hit Johnson in the neck. In an attempt to have his grenade detonate on impact, Bothwell had pulled the pin, released the handle, paused three seconds, then tossed it toward the enemy. The grenade, however, exploded in flight and rained fragments on the position. Russo was wounded in the hand and was unable to fire his M79. Bothwell radioed back to the command post informing them of the casualties; he then sprayed the area with M16 fire and, assisting Johnson and Russo, withdrew to the company position.

The wound in Johnson's neck, although not fatal, was very close to the jugular vein. The medical evacuation helicopter arrived twenty-five minutes later and evacuated the two men.

While the listening post was seeing action, an ambush patrol

PHASE II—THE HAMMER SWINGS

under Sergeant Julius Brown had been in position near the footpath. The patrol had left the command post at 1900 and moved south along the path, passing its ambush site and then backtracking to it to mislead any enemy elements following them. The ambush site had been chosen because of the cover available and the indications that the path was frequently traveled at this point. There were nine men in the patrol, six armed with M16's, two with M79's, and one with an M60 machine gun. The patrol maintained radio silence but was able to receive any messages transmitted to it. Captain Carney received reports from adjacent units that movement had been detected near their company command posts. He warned Sergeant Brown to keep on the alert for infiltrating Viet Cong.

At 1945 came the sounds of firing from Sergeant Bothwell's listening post. Shortly thereafter another warning of enemy activity in the area was received. The ambush patrol lay quietly waiting.

At 2045, sounds of movement were heard near the ambush site. Private First Class Gary Gaura became anxious and crawled to Sergeant Brown's position a few meters away to get instructions. Brown told him to do nothing and be still. When Gaura crawled back to his position, he coughed, and the enemy, now only about fifteen meters away, halted sharply. The Viet Cong remained silent and motionless for approximately ten minutes and then moved on around the patrol's killing zone. Private Gaura counted fifteen silhouettes. The enemy crossed the trail, avoiding the ambush, yet remained in the immediate area.

About one and a half hours later, the enemy column moved to the west and out of range and sight. Fifteen minutes later machine gun fire was heard from the direction of the adjacent company. At 2300 the sound of movement was again heard and out of the brush came a single enemy soldier. He cautiously moved toward the ambush position. Again someone coughed, alerting the enemy, but this time it was too late; there was no chance for escape. Private First Class Michael Farmer, armed with the M60 machine gun, squeezed off five rounds. The enemy fell wounded. Another enemy soldier emerged into the ambush site. He looked at the wounded man, turned, and walked away. The wounded man cried out. The straggler wheeled, sprayed the area with automatic weapons fire, and proceeded toward the man on the ground, walking so close to the ambush position that he nearly tripped over the barrel of the M60. Bending over, he lit a candle which illuminated both men. Private First Class Michael Hill fired his M60 machine gun but it malfunctioned; simultaneously Private First Class Martin Norman fired his M16. The candle went out.

Silence was maintained until morning when the two enemy dead were found along with two AK47 weapons. Among their personal items was a document containing codes for the Military Region IV headquarters; it appeared that the second Viet Cong had been a courier whose job was to transport important documents.

At 0630 the ambush patrol moved out of the area and returned to the company command post.

It later developed that the captured documents were one of the most significant finds of the operation and had a direct bearing on the subsequent capture of a high official assigned to Military Region IV.

CHAPTER V

The Hammer Strikes

Action proceeded in the Iron Triangle and Thanh Dien forest as the hammer continued its swing toward the anvil. On the morning of 11 January, General Seaman sent a message to the commanding generals of the 1st and 25th Divisions. After congratulating them on achieving initial surprise and on the encouraging results of the operation, he concluded by saying ". . . I want a thorough search to be made of the area of responsibility. . . . I particularly desire that the Iron Triangle be completely covered." It was in the spirit of this message that Operation CEDAR FALLS was conducted until its termination sixteen days later.

The operation was characterized by numerous small unit actions with both the hammer and anvil forces continuing to uncover increasingly large amounts of supplies. The men of the 1st and 25th Divisions searched meticulously, stripping the Iron Triangle and the surrounding area of all they could find that might be of value to the enemy. The enemy's defenses were weak and disorganized and had evidently been shattered by the mass and surprise of the attack. Mines, booby traps, and snipers were encountered, but there were no organized defenses or counterattacks. The enemy had evidently ordered units to disperse and try to escape. Because of the tight seal around the triangle, this was not always easy.

25th Infantry Division

Forces of the 25th Infantry Division continued search and destroy and search and clear operations along the Saigon River. The action was typified by company-size sweeps of assigned areas of operations. An entry in the 2d Brigade's after action report summarizes the activities of the 1st Battalion, 27th Infantry, on 17 January, which were fairly illustrative of the activities of the other units:

Co. A 1/27 conducted S&D [search and destroy] operations between AP NHA VIEC and the Saigon River. B 1/27 continued road clearing operations in sector. C 1/27 continued to outpost Saigon River. At 0947 hours A 1/27 destroyed one sampan, one bunker. At 1223 hours C 1/27 located 600 pounds rice. At 1350 hours C 1/27 destroyed four bunkers, and located miscellaneous documents. At 1515 hours A 1/27 destroyed three CBU's. At 1517 hours C 1/27 destroyed two bunkers. At 1531 hours A 1/27 located one VC KIA. At 1615 hours C 1/27 destroyed seven bunkers, six huts. At 1622 hours A 1/27 destroyed two bunkers. At 1720 hours A 1/27 destroyed two bunkers, one building, 200 pounds salt. At 2200 hours C 1/27 destroyed two sampans, two VC KIA (POSS).

The locations cited for these entries were all within one kilometer of the Saigon River in the vicinity of its junction with the Thi Tinh River.

The brigade elements also continued to work closely with the South Vietnamese 2d Battalion, 7th Regiment, in and around the village of Phu Hoa Dong.

Elements of the 25th Division continued to search the enemy base areas in the Ho Bo woods and Filhol Plantation while blocking enemy escape routes out of the Iron Triangle. Although most enemy contacts were with small scattered groups attempting to escape, one company did engage an enemy platoon and another destroyed a sampan with thirteen Viet Cong aboard. Buddy operations employing U.S. troops and the Vietnamese 5th River Assault Group patrolled both banks of the Saigon River to help seal off the triangle.

In accomplishing its objective of denying the enemy access to the Saigon River, the 25th Division employed various tactics, as described in a news release from the 25th Division's public information office:

CU CHI, VIETNAM (IO)—Part of the 25th Infantry Division's mission in Operation "Cedar Falls" was to seal off a portion of the Saigon River to all traffic. The Saigon River is a favorite escape route of the Viet Cong and the banks of the river are dotted with heavily fortified weapons emplacements.

"Tropic Lightning" soldiers used aerial observers and gunners and a waterborne force of RAG (River Assault Group) boats manned by infantrymen armed with automatic weapons and rifles. The RAG boats patrolled the river around the clock, raking the banks with their heavy firepower, while the gunships of the Division's D Troop, 3rd Squadron, 4th Cavalry, peppered fortifications and sampans alike with aerial rockets and machine gun fire.

As the operation continued, the Viet Cong began to realize that the airborne-waterborne, one-two punch made the Saigon River a boundary they could not afford to come near, let alone cross.

Even at night the river was sealed. The RAG boats used searchlights to probe the darkened shoreline, and tanks used their high intensity Xenon lights to scan the water and the aviation units used the firefly team with a 1,750,000 candlepower beam to scan both areas. With these tools, very little escaped their surveillance.

Despite the destruction and sporadic contact which were occurring, the division forces found the time and occasion for civic

MEMBERS OF COMPANY C., 1ST BATTALION, 27TH INFANTRY, PATROLLING THE SAIGON RIVER

action activities, as noted in the following extracts from the after action report of the 2d Brigade, 25th Infantry Division:

11 Jan 1967 . . . 2d Bn, 27th Infantry . . .
A MEDCAP [Medical Civic Action Program] was conducted on the outskirts of forward base camp and 38 patients were treated. This number is not impressive except that the people in this area had been indoctrinated by the VC that American medicine would harm them. One woman had an ill child but would not let the doctor give it medicine. Several days later this woman returned and allowed the child to be given medicine since she had seen that the medicine did not harm others who had taken it. On 11 Jan the MEDCAP also distributed candy and toys to the children.

15 Jan 1967 . . . 2d Bn, 27th Infantry . . .
Civic Action: MEDCAP operations were again conducted at base camp, where 163 patients were treated. This, it should be noted, was a tremendous increase over the first day's total of 38 patients, and indicates the continued progress in gaining the respect of the local civilians.

To the north of the 25th Division's 2d Brigade, the 196th Light Infantry Brigade was conducting similar operations in its area of responsibility. Using patrols, company-size search and destroy operations, and periodic platoon airmobile assaults, the brigade uncovered numerous installations containing caches of enemy munitions, food, clothing, documents, and equipment. One company reported during this time that it had "engaged 14 bushes floating upstream resulting in 10 VC KIA (Possible)."

Another low-key report was submitted on 18 January by the 1st Battalion, 5th Infantry, and stated simply: "At 1730 hours Company A discovered an extensive tunnel complex." However, it developed that this discovery probably uncovered the headquarters of Military Region IV or at least a significant portion of it.

The tunnel system was located adjacent to the stream (the Rach Son) which marked the 196th Light Infantry's south boundary, on a narrow strip of relatively clear land between the Ho Bo woods and the Filhol Plantation. In the first few hours after its discovery, the vast complex yielded forty pounds of documents including detailed maps of Saigon and the Tan Son Nhut area, maps showing the schemes of maneuver of friendly operations in the area and Viet Cong routes of movement from the Iron Triangle area to the Saigon River.

Newsweek magazine described the tunnel discovery in these words:

> Entering the shaft head first through a small hole that descended to the tunnel floor some 16 feet below, the tunnel rats spread out through the winding galleries. Soon they realized they were on to something big. In their haste to escape, the Viet Cong had left behind not only medical supplies and weapons but maps, diagrams of U.S. billets in Saigon and other plans for terrorists raids. One of the documents outlined the plan for the December 4 raid on Tan Son Nhut air base. Brigadier General Richard Knowles, commander of the 196th, was clearly convinced that his men had found the headquarters for all Viet Cong activity in the Saigon region. "This is by far the most important one yet," said Knowles last week. "This was his headquarters."

Company A, together with other elements of the battalion, searched the tunnels during the next six days. *Time* magazine related the story of the complex's end:

> There were a few Viet Cong defenders left behind, and the G.I.s, equipped with silencer-mounted .38 pistols, pursued them through the labyrinth. After exploring the maze for 1,000 yards, the tunnel rats came up and turned the task over to units that pumped riot control agents through the system, then set about blasting it to dust.

Small villages in the area were searched and cleared. Armed helicopters, used deceptively, orbited the villages before the ground forces moved in, as described by General Knowles:

> Armed helicopters proved to be extremely valuable in search and clear

operations of villages. It was observed on CEDAR FALLS that armed helicopters on station would prevent the VC from fleeing the village into the rice paddies. Once armed helicopters would leave the area, it was discovered the VC would try to make their escape from the village being searched. One technique which proved successful was to have the armed helicopters leave the village area for four to five minutes. The VC, thinking the helicopters had left for good, would then try to make their escape. The helicopters would then return and observe the VC fleeing and take them under fire.

The 196th Light Infantry Brigade terminated Operation CEDAR FALLS on 25 January when the last elements left the operational area and closed at their Tay Ninh base camp. The organic battalion of the 25th Division which had been attached to the 196th was released and moved overland to Cu Chi, the base camp of the 25th Division. However, the 25th Division's operations had proved so profitable that elements of the 2d Brigade continued to search the area as part of Operation ALA MOANA after the termination of CEDAR FALLS on 26 January.

1st Infantry Division

On 10 January two South Vietnamese battalions relieved the 1st Squadron, 4th Cavalry, of its security mission along the Thi Tinh River, and the squadron came under the operational control of the 11th Armored Cavalry Regiment (and Task Force DEANE) and took over the blocking assignments of the 2d and 4th Battalions, 503d Infantry, along the east side of the Thanh Dien forest perimeter. The following day these two battalions, under the control of Task Force DEANE, turned southward.

Having been relieved of the Ben Suc seal mission by the two South Vietnamese airborne battalions on 10 January, the 1st Battalion, 26th Infantry, still under the 2d Brigade, was committed on the next day to assisting in the search of the Thanh Dien forest.

1st Division forces combed the enemy sanctuary throughout the remaining days of the operation and found huge quantities of rice, hundreds of documents, and many enemy weapons and much ammunition; destroyed enemy tunnels and bunkers; and stripped trees and underbrush from roads and trails and carved out landing zones for future operations. By 12 January 1st Division forces had captured 1,800 tons of rice, 189 small arms, and 971 grenades. The 1st Battalion, 2d Infantry, had located a 100-bed underground hospital complete with blankets and equipment along the northwestern edge of the Thanh Dien forest.

The two battalions of the 503d Infantry attacked south into the triangle, with units of the 11th Armored Cavalry Regiment screening on the north and augmenting the infantry battalions in search

TANKERS FROM THE 1ST SQUADRON, 4TH CAVALRY, *in a rubber plantation.*

and destroy missions. Based upon its experience in the triangle, the Blackhorse Regiment reported a new approach to the discovery of rice caches:

> During Operation CEDAR FALLS it was observed that anytime a large cache of rice had been discovered a flock of small birds had been frightened away by the approach of friendly troops. Accordingly, any time a flock of birds was noticed, a search for a rice cache was made in the area.

Only light and occasional contact continued with the enemy while the task force moved south uncovering quantities of material and numerous fortifications.

As the operation continued, the number of enemy *Chieu Hoi* (open arms) ralliers grew well beyond previous totals. Psychological Operations field teams effectively exploited these ralliers by printing rapid reaction leaflets containing surrender appeals from the ralliers to their Viet Cong friends. Typical of the messages dropped was one written by rallier Le Van Sa. Printed on both sides of 5x8-inch paper, 50,000 copies were disseminated in the 1st Infantry Division's area of operations:

> To my dear friends still in the VC Ranks, I am Le Van Sa, medic of the medical team of VH (MB 3011). I followed the VC by their false inducement. I found fault with our people and nation. I have gone the wrong way. But in time I found out what is right and what is wrong. I have rallied to the GVN and have been warmly welcomed, well treated. At the present time I am very happy at the CH (Chieu Hoi) Center. I also saw my family who are living in the Resettlement Center of GVN. I send to you this letter so that you too could rally to the Government side where you can start a new life and see your families. My dear friends: Hung, Rong, Tieng, Chi, Tu Dan, Minh Nhan, Tha Luong, Tam Thu, Thanh, Huyen, Lion, Thau, Mong Tieng, Ut and Gan, all of you should return to GVN as soon as possible. Saying with VC, you will have no place to hide. You can use any Chieu Hoi leaflet and take the nearest road to report to the Government or Allied Military Installations. You will be treated as we are now. There are more than 300 VC who have returned to the National Just Cause in a very short time. They are having a good living here at the CH Center. They have been well treated. My dear friends you should rally right now to avoid useless deaths. Tet is going to come very soon. Rally to reunite with your families. The door of the Chieu Hoi Center is wide open for your return.

The leaflet also bore a photograph of Sa.

In addition to these quick reaction messages directed at individual Viet Cong by name, more general messages were also dropped encouraging the Viet Cong to give up. One such message read:

> To VC of South Ben Cat, the powerful GVN and Allied Forces will continue extensive operations in the area of Ben Suc and south Ben Cat. All base camps will be destroyed and the area will be subjected to continuous artillery fire and air strikes. Huge areas of jungle are being removed and there will be no safety for VC anywhere. You will no longer find shelter or supplies here, and you will not have safe base camps. All VC remaining in this area will meet inevitable death.
>
> From 8 to 15 Jan 67, 259 of your comrades have been killed and 60 captured, and numerous other supplies, clothing and equipment have been captured or destroyed.
>
> More than 200 of your comrades have already rallied to the GVN and are receiving good treatment. Rally now and start a new life of happiness, united with your families. Turn yourself in to the nearest government office. A government office is located in Ben Cat where you will be welcomed with open arms and given protection. Walk to any road that leads to Ben Cat—stay on the road—walk at all times—if you run your intentions may be mistaken and you may be killed. Use the sketch map on the back of this leaflet as your guide to safety and freedom. Rally now before it is too late!

On the reverse side of the 5x8-inch sheet was a map of the Iron Triangle.

Over five hundred Viet Cong surrendered during the operation, many as a result of the Psychological Operations but most because the continued presence of allied troops gave them no choice when they became hungry, wet, and out of supplies and support.

AMERICAN AND VIETNAMESE SOLDIERS OF THE 1ST INFANTRY DIVISION AND 5TH ARVN DIVISION *assist refugees at the town of Bung Cong, near the Saigon River.*

The evacuation of civilians from Ben Suc and the other three villages in the triangle continued through 16 January. About half of the inhabitants made the journey to the Phu Cuong resettlement camp in Chinook helicopters or South Vietnamese Navy craft down the Saigon River. After the road from Ben Cat to Ben Suc via Rach Bap was passable, the other 3,000 traveled by truck convoy. This unprecedented mass evauacation, executed on short notice, required a tremendous effort by U.S. and South Vietnamese military and civilian agencies; but it would be weeks before the latter could restore a sense of normality to the evacuees. Eventually they would have their own village with its school, raise their own crops with access to the Saigon markets, and have much-needed medical assistance available. Meanwhile, a source of supply and support for the Viet Cong had been eliminated.

By 14 January the forces of the 1st Division were starting gradually to wind down CEDAR FALLS. However, before they did, the Blue Spaders of the 1st Battalion, 26th Infantry, moving to the northwest of Ben Suc, uncovered one of the more highly developed and strongly built enemy complexes to be found in the area located less than one kilometer from the Saigon River. This is the description of it contained in the after action report of the Big Red One's 2d Brigade:

> Building #1 was approximately 9 feet wide by 18 feet long and 10 feet below the surface of the ground. The building had cement on all four sides and flooring about 5 inches thick. The only overhead protection was afforded by sheets of tin. On the northwest corner was a bunker with no overhead protection. Beds and tables were on the floor.
>
> Build #2 was approximately 9 feet wide by 12 feet long and 10 feet below the surface. It had concrete identical to Building #1. Overhead cover over one-half of the structure consisted of 5 inch logs and 3 feet of packed dirt. There were no fighting positions located near the building and beds were located on the 1st floor and on top of the overhead protection. Building #3 and #4 were exactly identical to building #2.
>
> Bunker #5 located north of the camp and connected by tunnel to building #3 had overhead protection of 5 inch logs and 3 feet of packed dirt. There were four firing apertures, each 2 inches high and 4-6 inches wide and each could cover an area over 100m wide to the front.
>
> The second level tunnel going north was made so that at every 10-15m it came to a dead end; and a trap door on the floor connected with a tunnel which went down, around and back up to the other side and on the same level with the fake dead end. There were two small holes in the dead end permitting one man to observe and fire through the tunnel.

On 17 January the 2d Brigade ended its participation in CEDAR FALLS. By 18 January the 3d Brigade had withdrawn. Task Force DEANE terminated CEDAR FALLS on 25 January while the 1st Squadron, 4th Cavalry, continued road security in the triangle for the departing engineer work parties. At midnight, 26 January 1967, the operation came to a close.

CHAPTER VI

Engineer and Chemical Operations

Starting with the construction of the D. S. [double-single] Bailey Bridge at Ben Cat on 21 Dec 66, and ending with the demolition of the tunnel complexes on 26 Jan 67, Operation Cedar Falls was without exception the most significant combat engineering operation of the war to date. New concepts of jungle warfare using dozers to open heretofore inviolable VC strongholds; the emergence of a new "Secret Weapon," the dozer-infantry teams; and combined acetylene and HE (High Explosive) tunnel demolitions; all have proven unique, successful, and of tremendous value to future operations. Operations Niagara Falls and Cedar Falls introduced massive jungle clearing in conjunction with tactical infantry operation on a scale never attempted before. A total of 54 bulldozers were under the OPCON (Operation Control) of the 1st Engineer Battalion. . . .

So spoke Lieutenant Colonel Joseph M. Kiernan, Jr., commanding officer of the 1st Engineer Battalion, in summarizing engineer operations during CEDAR FALLS.

Engineer and chemical operations during CEDAR FALLS involved innovative techniques as well as others more familiar and routine. Engineer forces were assigned normal missions such as the construction of a 160-foot Bailey bridge before the operation to facilitate the movement of the 11th Armored Cavalry Regiment into the Iron Triangle and the clearing and construction of landing zones, roads, and support areas. More unusual projects included the clearing and destruction of enemy underground complexes during search and destroy operations, the stripping of acres of jungle, and the establishment of a waterborne seal at the confluence of the Saigon and Thi Tinh Rivers to prevent enemy escape. The dropping of CS munitions from helicopters and the destruction of rice were entrusted to the chemical personnel.

The engineer–chemical task force for CEDAR FALLS had under Colonel Kiernan's command some six hundred men from the 1st Engineer Battalion, flamethrower platoons from the 1st Squadron, 4th Cavalry, the "tunnel rats" (tunnel exploration and demolition crews) from the 242d Chemical Detachment, and approximately three hundred engineers from the 79th Engineer Group. This last complement consisted of men and equipment drawn from four engineer battalions, a light equipment company, and a maintenance detachment.

Bridge on the Thi Tinh

To provide rapid crossing for the 11th Armored Cavalry Regiment and supporting forces as they launched their sweep from Ben Cat toward objectives on the opposite side of the Iron Triangle, the 1st Engineer Battalion of the Big Red One was directed to construct a Bailey bridge over the Thi Tinh River just west of Ben Cat. Work commenced on 21 December, well before D-day, at a site adjacent to an existing Eiffel bridge and a destroyed concrete bridge. The bridge site preparation included the destruction of the remains of the concrete bridge, the construction of headwalls on each bank, and the construction of an eight-pile pier in the center of the river to support the 80-foot Bailey bridge sections. The assembly of the bridge was begun on 31 December, the launch made on 1 January, and the final welding done by 5 January.

Disaster struck the new bridge on the afternoon of 9 January when a recovery vehicle towing a disabled M-48 tank crashed through the western span. All traffic was halted and an emergency repair crew of the battalion was directed to remove both vehicles from the river and replace the damaged span temporarily with an AVLB (armored vehicle launched bridge). The Eiffel bridge, which had also been damaged by the collapse of the Bailey, was reinforced and opened by 1630, although limited to medium truck traffic. To launch the AVLB, the Bailey span had to be removed from the pier and disassembled—a difficult and time-consuming task. The western approach was extended twenty feet by earth fill and was bolstered by damaged Bailey parts. The shorter (60-foot) AVLB was successfully launched by 0515 the next morning. The bridge was opened to traffic at daybreak.

Jungle Clearing Operations

During late December 1966 and early January 1967, the engineer task force structure and support role in preparation for the vast amount of jungle clearing for CEDAR FALLS were developed and partially tested in Operation NIAGARA FALLS. The tractor assets from the engineer battalions of the 79th Engineer Group were consolidated under the headquarters of one of its battalions, the 168th, to support the 1st Infantry Division. Experience in NIAGARA FALLS had revealed that the tractors must have an "in-house" maintenance capability to provide on-the-spot servicing and small repairs; thus, a composite maintenance task force was organized. There also was an attachment from a maintenance battalion which could fabricate parts. Unit and tractor-type integrity was maintained by dividing the personnel and equipment into teams.

ROME PLOW IN OPERATION

The decision was made to employ the dozer-infantry team. Tankdozers, bulldozers, Rome Plows,* and the infantry would cut into the enemy-infested jungle together, simultaneously clearing the area of vegetation, conducting search and destroy operations, and destroying enemy fortifications.

The dozer-infantry teams used two techniques based upon the tactical situation and the basic characteristics of the equipment. One was a formation of two tankdozers at the point, followed by four bulldozers abreast, with two more dozers as a cleanup team to

---

*A tankdozer is an M-48 medium tank with a bulldozer blade. The heavy armor provides protection from most mines, booby traps, and snipers; the tankdozer is a favored leading vehicle during jungle clearing operations. The Rome Plow is a large tractor with a specially configured dozer-type blade developed specifically for heavy-duty land clearing operations, civilian and military, by the Rome Caterpillar Company of Rome, Georgia. The blade is more curved than the usual bulldozer blade and has a protruding, sharply honed lower edge. The lower edge curves out on one side to form a spike used to split trees too large to cut with the blade alone, but the blade itself can slice a tree of three feet in diameter. Bars are added to the top of the blade to force trees away from the tractor, and there is a safety feature—a "headache bar"—over the operator's position to protect him from falling debris. Some Rome Plows were also modified to include light armor for the operator.

PREPARING LANDING ZONE

windrow the vegetation that had been cut. Infantry supported the tractors, at the same time carrying out search and destroy missions. The second technique employed a Rome Plow in the lead followed by troops in armored vehicles. When contact with the enemy was made, the men in the vehicles provided fire support until the accompanying infantry could silence the enemy.

A significant advantage of the dozer-infantry team was the additional time it gave the infantry to conduct search and destroy operations. During previous jungle operations the infantry often had been forced to stop to clear resupply landing zones by hand. With the dozers along they could do the clearing, and do it in minutes.

The test of the jungle clearing concepts in NIAGARA FALLS had revealed that the three or four weeks planned for CEDAR FALLS were not adequate to clear the entire jungle in the Iron Triangle. Instead, only 7 or 8 percent of the sixty-three square miles of jungle area could be cleared in that time. Therefore, only strategic areas such as those along roads and landing zones would be cleared, plus

Engineers Rappelling off Helicopter

spaced swaths to permit rapid deployment by mechanized and airmobile units in future operations. The swaths were defined as the operation progressed.

The CEDAR FALLS clearing operations commenced on the afternoon of D plus 1, 9 January, the same day that three engineer base camps were scratched out of the north side of the triangle and spaced along the eight kilometers of road between Ben Cat and Rach Bap. A half mile of clearing along the roadway, fifty meters wide, was also cut that first day. On the following day over 3,300 meters of jungle were torn apart. Also on the second day an engineer platoon with the mission of clearing a landing zone scrambled down the 70-foot ladder from a Chinook hovering over the jungle and joined the 1st Battalion, 28th Infantry, in the Thanh Dien forest. Two hours later the landing zone was ready to receive the first helicopter; later it was enlarged to accommodate four at a time.

In this operation as in most utilizing a large amount of heavy mechanical equipment, the two major problems were fuel resupply and vehicle maintenance. Each dozer team consumed 600 gallons

INSPECTING AN ENEMY BOOBY TRAP

of diesel fuel per day. Usually at least six refueling locations—some supplied solely by 500-gallon pods brought in by air—were required daily. Several teams had to be supplied on site by air. When field pumps were in short supply, trenches eight feet deep were dug and the fuel was gravity-fed from the top of the cut into the vehicles. Maintenance problems were compounded by the quantity of equipment involved and the distances between teams. Repairs were made in the field whenever possible; otherwise the disabled vehicle was moved by truck to Lai Khe where heavy maintenance support was provided by elements of the 79th Engineer Group. The maintenance task force operated around the clock and was the significant factor in achieving the very low deadline rate (percentage of vehicles not usable because of needed maintenance) of 10 to 15 percent for tractors and dozers throughout the operation.

Engineer clearing operations continued until 22 January with some impressive results. The jungle area cleared totaled 2,711 acres or 10.9 square kilometers, including 50 to 100 meters of jungle on each side of the major roads in the Iron Triangle as well as 34 landing zones tactically spaced throughout the triangle. Three of the

Searching for Tunnels

zones were cleared by engineers lifted into the jungle by helicopter, the remainder by dozer-infantry teams. In addition, numerous swaths were cut through the jungle, usually in widths from 50 to 100 meters. During the clearing, many small engagements occurred between the engineers and enemy snipers, and, in one instance, an enemy squad. Numerous booby traps were also encountered. However, the 1st Engineer Battalion had only 1 man killed and 7 wounded by hostile action during the operation, while the supporting engineer units had 7 wounded.

Tunnel Exploration and Destruction

Enemy combat units generally did not use tunnel systems. Rather, as do most military forces, they relied on fighting positions, trenches, and bunkers for protection. Tunnel systems were dug by those relatively stationary Viet Cong elements such as village and hamlet cadres, logistical units, and headquarters elements. Consequently, tunnels were most often found in the enemy-controlled villages and logistical base areas but not necessarily in combat unit base camps. Interrogated prisoners and returnees revealed that as a rule personnel of organized Viet Cong combat units did not know the location of such tunnels. They might frequently reveal the general location, but information to locate the tunnels precisely had to come usually from local cadres and rear service personnel.

Extensive tunnel systems were found throughout the Iron Triangle–Thanh Dien forest area. Operation CEDAR FALLS demonstrated that patience is the primary weapon to use against an enemy hiding in tunnels: wait for him to run out of supplies or to get curious about where you are or what you are doing. It was sometimes necessary to flush the enemy out with tunnel rats or riot control agents or to seal and destroy the tunnels.

A tunnel rat team usually consisted of from six to ten men led by an officer or a noncommissioned officer. The individual in charge had the responsibility of drawing a sketch of the underground complex from information relayed from the team members within the tunnel. The lead element of the tunnel rat team was usually armed with a pistol equipped with a silencer (to fire in a tunnel without a silencer was to risk broken eardrums), hand telephone or "skull mike," flashlight, compass, and probe. One of the major problems in tunnel reconnaissance was that of communications. The skull mike (a transmitter strapped to the back of the skull) often became inoperative after a short period. In addition, the heavier U.S. communications wire which had to be used in lieu of the scarce lightweight Canadian assault wire added considerable weight and bulk to the team. Lack of fresh air was also a problem for the men when deep in the tunnels. The "Mighty Mite" (an air compressor with blower) or an auxiliary helicopter engine rigged with a 50- to 100-foot length of hose was often employed to force fresh air into the tunnel systems.

The job of a tunnel rat was difficult at best. Hot, dirty, and gasping for breath, he squeezed his body through narrow and shallow openings on all fours, never knowing whether the tunnel might collapse behind him or what he might find ahead around the next turn, and sensing the jolt of adrenalin at every sound. Surely this modern combat spelunker is a special breed.

The following is a description of the search and destruction of a large tunnel complex located in the triangle approximately six kilometers south of Rach Bap and about six hundred meters to the east of Route 14.

On 21 January a Viet Cong sympathizer was apprehended by the 168th Engineers and admitted having helped dig the underground complex. A patrol was organized from the staff sections of the 1st Engineer Battalion and was led by the sympathizer to the tunnel area where he pointed out several air holes and firing ports. Further examination of the area uncovered a base camp with several tunnel entrances.

The next day, after posting security forces, a thorough search of the tunnels was begun by engineer tunnel rats with initial negative results. Then a breather hole was blown open revealing the entrance to hundreds of meters of additional tunnel. About six hundred meters into the tunnel the engineers ran into an accumulation of CS, and the exploration stopped. The many documents found in the complex were taken to the G-2 of the 1st Division; upon evaluation of the papers, the G-2 determined that the search of the tunnel complex should be continued.

Next day the engineer tunnel rats returned accompanied by their counterparts from the attached chemical platoon. After exploring an additional 800 meters of tunnel, they found and removed a trapdoor, disclosing additional chambers and documents. Over one kilometer of tunnel had now been uncovered. Further exploration revealed an exit leading to another enemy base camp.

The exploration continued the following day, and more documents were uncovered and evacuated. As the tunnel rats crawled through the complex, they heard enemy voices. A CS grenade thrown by the team flushed five Viet Cong from the tunnel; they were captured as they scrambled out. Above ground, the security elements found a former hospital base camp complex 300 meters north of the camp discovered the previous day, and an investigation of tunnels of this complex was begun.

Early the next morning, the fourth day of exploration, the tunnel rats returned to the former hospital complex. Five huts were unearthed, each dug into the ground so that the roof was at ground level. Medical textbooks and notebooks, small quantities of medicine, and medical instruments were discovered in the 300 meters of rooms and chambers. The tunnel team returned to the second tunnel complex where the Viet Cong had been flushed, but CS in the tunnel prevented further exploration. Tunnel destruction personnel from the 168th Engineers arrived that afternoon and remained at the overnight position.

On 26 January, the day CEDAR FALLS terminated, the tunnel destruction team left for the former hospital complex and the exploration team returned to the "CS tunnel" complex. Using conventional demolitions and acetylene equipment, the team rigged the hospital complex for destruction after receiving word that no additional information had been found by those combing the underground labyrinth. The charges were detonated at noon; after the explosion, large cracks could be seen on the surface for a distance of approximately two hundred meters. The team then moved to the second tunnel complex and, again using a combination of conventional demolitions and acetylene, destroyed it.

Because of the numerous enemy underground complexes discovered, there were too many burrows for the few trained tunnel rats to explore. Volunteers from the 1st Engineers and other units often took on the task of exploration and destruction. As would be expected, the results when using trained, experienced, and properly equipped personnel were much more valuable—and far safer—than those gained through volunteers. Unless the tunnel was mapped as it was explored, the engineers who were to destroy the tunnel were required to go back in and map it, duplicating effort. There were also instances in which two teams were in a tunnel at the same time with neither team knowing of the other's presence. Luckily, no one was shot by mistake.

A new method of tunnel destruction was developed and used during CEDAR FALLS. It consisted of filling a tunnel with acetylene gas—forced in by blowers—then igniting the gas by demolition charges. Acetylene alone was found excellent for destroying tunnels with not more than seven feet of overhead cover. With deeper tunnels destruction was increased through the use of conventional demolitions in conjunction with the acetylene. Thirty-pound charges of TNT and 40-pound cratering charges were placed at critical locations (rooms, tunnel junctions, exits, and entrances) in the complex. These charges were dual primed, connected in series by detonation cord, and fired electrically. When detonated, the conventional charges acted as booster charges for the acetylene. These experiments, using high explosives and acetylene together, proved very effective on tunnels as much as fifteen to twenty feet below the surface.

During Operation CEDAR FALLS the 1st Engineers and attached units discovered literally helicopter loads of documents, records, and plans, many of which belonged to the Viet Cong intelligence section of Military Region IV from 1963 through 1966. The documents listed the strengths of Viet Cong units, the names of their members, and the towns and villages in which they operated; disclosed some of their meeting places; and revealed a great amount of information on exactly how the enemy operated and what his future plans were. In addition to intelligence gathering and jungle destruction, 9,445 meters of enemy tunnels, 4 villages, 27 base camps, 60 miscellaneous bunkers, and other facilities were destroyed by the engineers.

The Engineer Navy

The problem of sealing the confluence of the Saigon and Thi Tinh Rivers in order to prevent the escape of the Viet Cong by water during CEDAR FALLS resulted in another new approach to counterinsurgency warfare, an engineer "navy." The initial plan to deny this escape route to the enemy was to place a force on the banks of each of the rivers. The force would be armed with the newly acquired "quad-.50" machine guns (four heavy machine guns that traverse from a single pedestal and which are fired simultaneously by one gunner). General DePuy believed this mission could be more efficiently accomplished by installing the quad-.50's on platforms placed in the river. The engineers agreed and were given the job.

On 3 January Company E, 1st Engineer Battalion, was directed to procure and load the materials for two rafts to support the weapons and to move the materials to the Vietnamese Engineer School at Phu Cuong, twelve kilometers downstream from the juncture of the Saigon and Thi Tinh Rivers. There each raft was built by connecting two bridge floats with aluminum decking, and a quad-.50 was mounted on each of the platforms. The construction was completed in one day. Additional firepower for each raft was provided by six .30-caliber machine guns, and provision was made for riflemen and grenadiers behind sandbags to be on both the floats and the platform. Eventually dubbed Monitors, each raft was propelled by a 27-foot utility boat.

The navy also included two armed utility boats and several river patrols using pneumatic assault boats. The river patrols consisted of fifteen men: two engineers and thirteen infantrymen. One engineer operated the boat while the other secured it during loading and unloading.

Early on 5 January, with a command helicopter overhead, the engineer flotilla left Phu Cuong and moved up the Saigon River. Approximately two kilometers from its destination, lead elements experienced sniper fire which was immediately countered by machine guns from the rafts and the helicopter; four enemy were killed. By nightfall the rafts were in position at the confluence of the rivers; one raft tied to the east bank and the other anchored in midstream.

While the Monitors remained in the same general vicinity for most of the operation, the utility and assault boats actively patrolled the rivers. All Vietnamese river traffic was checked and some prisoners taken. In addition the boats ferried supplies to outposts along the river. The navy of the 1st Engineers proved to be a great asset during CEDAR FALLS.

Chemical Operations

During CEDAR FALLS the chemical sections of both the 1st Division and 173d Airborne Brigade were used to achieve excellent results in combat operations and in denying materiel and facilities to the enemy.

On 8 January the 1st Division chemical section conducted an experimental drop of 55-gallon drums of CS munitions from a CH-47 (Chinook) helicopter in the Thanh Dien forest in the 3d Brigade's area of operation. On 13 January another drop of thirty drums of CS set to explode at treetop level was made on a linear target approximately fifteen hundred meters long just south of Artillery Base I. Excellent functioning of the explosives and coverage of the target were reported by the Air Force forward air controller observing the drop. On 16 January another 30-drum drop was made on an enemy base camp outside of the CEDAR FALLS operational area. To produce better results on this broad target, two passes were made forming an X with fifteen drums dropped on each pass. Good coverage was again reported. Two more drops were made outside the CEDAR FALLS area the next day, again with excellent results. Such drops, when made under controlled conditions in territory in friendly hands, kept the enemy from entering the area of the drop for many days unless he was masked.

The chemical sections were also very active and effective in denying use of captured rice to the enemy. When conditions permitted, the rice was removed from the area. However, in some cases, in view of the large tonnages involved as well as the location of the rice, removal was impossible. For example, on 12 January 450 tons of rice in 100-pound bags, located in eight different caches, were destroyed by the chemical personnel of the 1st Division. To contaminate the rice, a hole was made in the middle of the cache and two 40-pound cratering charges were placed in the hole and detonated. The explosion caused the bags to burst and spread the rice over a wide area. Eight-pound bags of CS crystals were then placed in and around the area, linked with detonating cord, and exploded simultaneously. This system was often and effectively used during the operation.

FLAMETHROWER IN ACTION

Flamethrowers were also employed during Operation CEDAR FALLS for land clearing and against entrenched enemy troops. Flamethrowers provided the best means of destroying the windrows of trees and brush caused by jungle clearing operations. The flamethrower-equipped tracked vehicles of the 1st Squadron, 4th Cavalry, were used to burn the green jungle which had been cut. It was found that 2,600 gallons of diesel fuel, 1,500 gallons of gasoline, and 1,500 pounds of chemicals were required to consume four windrows, each 50 meters long. This expensive operation was used rather sparingly. The 2d Brigade also employed flamethrowers to assist in the capture of Viet Cong located in bunkers and tunnels. The flamethrowers reduced the amount of oxygen in the tunnels, to say nothing of producing a significantly adverse psychological effect on the enemy.

The main support of the tunnel search effort by the chemical sections, in addition to the actual tunnel rat teams, consisted of providing different types of air blowers for various uses. One use was to blow smoke into tunnels which had been located (especially those with extremely small diameters whiich were impractical or too difficult to search) to flush out any Viet Cong and to locate other entrances, gun ports, or breathing holes. The Buffalo Turbine, a powerful blower, was often used for this purpose along with 30-pound smoke pots. To assist in locating the smoke exiting the tunnels, observation helicopters as well as troops scouted the area. Because the smoke did not linger, the tunnels could be flushed by the blowers with relative ease so that tunnel rats could almost immediately search the tunnel. On 19 January this kind of smoke operation caused seven Viet Cong to flee a tunnel in the area of operations of the 2d Battalion, 503d Infantry. All were immediately apprehended, suffering from the effects of smoke inhalation. However, after an hour of flushing the tunnel with fresh air, a tunnel rat team was able to search the tunnel with no difficulty. At times the blowers were also used to fill the tunnels with CS.

The Army engineers and chemical teams contributed significantly to the task of destroying the enemy's facilities in the Iron Triangle and making its future use difficult. As *Time* magazine put it as CEDAR FALLS was drawing to a close, "If the U.S. has its way, even a crow flying across the Triangle will have to carry lunch from now on."

CHAPTER VII

The Results

During its 19-day duration CEDAR FALLS compiled some impressive statistics. U.S. and South Vietnamese forces accounted for nearly 750 confirmed enemy dead and 280 prisoners. In addition, there were 540 Viet Cong *Chieu Hoi* ralliers, 512 suspects detained, and 5,987 refugees evacuated. Enemy equipment losses were 23 crew-served weapons, 590 individual weapons, and over 2,800 explosive items such as mines, grenades, and mortar and artillery rounds. Over 60,000 rounds of small arms ammunition were captured, as were many miscellaneous items of equipment, including over 7,500 uniforms. Some 1,100 bunkers, 525 tunnels, and over 500 structures were destroyed. Captured were 3,700 tons of rice—enough to feed 13,000 troops for a full year—and more than a half million pages of assorted documents.

U.S. battle losses totaled 72 killed, 337 wounded; those for the South Vietnamese, 11 killed and 8 wounded. U.S. equipment lost included 1 tank and 3 armored personnel carriers (APC's). Damage was sustained by 3 tanks, 9 APC's, 1 tankdozer, 2 quarter-ton trucks (jeeps), and 2 light observation helicopters. The South Vietnamese lost 3 individual weapons.

In addition, eleven square kilometers of jungle were cleared and many miles of road in the area were made passable. These roads, the landing zones cleared, and the swaths cut at intervals through the jungle would all make any future penetration of the area much simpler.

As had been expected, main force elements were contacted only rarely. The 1st, 7th, and 8th Viet Cong Main Force Battalions of Military Region IV did not conduct an organized defense of their areas, apparently having been directed to disperse and avoid contact. Task Force DEANE did report prisoners taken from the 61st Local Force Company of the Phu Loi Battalion and from small rear services elements.

A review of the interrogation reports of those who rallied, were taken prisoner, or detained indicated that the majority were from Viet Cong infrastructure in the area. Over three hundred of the ralliers and prisoners were from local guerrilla units, primarily

COMBINED ARMS—INFANTRY, ARMOR, AND AIR—AT WORK IN THE IRON TRIANGLE

from Ben Cat District. Personnel from combat support elements, such as farmers and laborers, accounted for the second largest category, about 25 percent. Only a few top-level cadres were identified in interrogation reports, including an executive officer of Tay Ninh Military School, a captain from the Military Region IV political staff section, a lieutenant from a small guard unit, and two North Vietnamese political cadres, including the mathematics professor schooled at Peking University.

It appeared from the near-total absence of enemy acts of sabotage or attacks on government posts in or around Saigon during the operation that the grasp of the infrastructure upon the former inhabitants of the Iron Triangle area had been severely impaired. General Westmoreland, in commenting on CEDAR FALLS during a Mission Council meeting, stated that the operation had been a very disruptive one for the enemy in the Iron Triangle area. He added that it had been very impressive in its results, being the first operation in which the number of enemy captured and detained equaled the number of enemy killed.

AMERICAN ADVISER AND VIETNAMESE SOLDIERS *keeping watch on Viet Cong captives.*

In analyzing CEDAR FALLS, General Seaman discussed the operation from several aspects. With respect to surprise, he wrote:

Security in planning and deception in deployment resulted in surprising the enemy. The light initial contact and the lack of a well-coordinated defense indicated that not only did the enemy not expect our attack but was unable to react when it came. The final casualty figures show that he had been in the Iron Triangle in considerable strength, despite his weak defense.

General Seaman pointed out that application of the principle of mass had quickly and effectively sealed and thoroughly searched the area of operations by using a higher troop density than had ever before been used or been possible. This greatly improved the effectiveness of cordon and search tactics and was reflected in the high proportion of Viet Cong ralliers. "Not being able to hide or escape," he indicated, "their choice was to surrender."

General Knowles of the 196th Brigade highlighted another factor which contributed to more ralliers than before: CEDAR FALLS was a longer operation than most.

THE RESULTS

Operation CEDAR FALLS demonstrated the value of extended operations within VC controlled areas. The length of the operation gave the small unit commanders and the troops time enough to become familiar with the terrain, as well as the VC situation. Unlike many other operations where troops go into an area for two or three day search and destroy missions, CEDAR FALLS provided the much needed continuity of effort to effectively accomplish the mission.

General Knowles also directed the following comments at the critics of mechanized units being used in counterinsurgency operations:

Mechanized infantry has proven to be highly successful in search and destroy operations. With their capability for rapid reaction and firepower, a mechanized battalion can effectively control twice as much terrain as an infantry battalion. Rapid penetrations into VC controlled areas to secure LZ's for airmobile units provides an added security measure for aircraft as well as personnel when introducing units into the combat zone. The constant movement of mech units back and forth through an area keeps the VC moving and creates targets for friendly ambushes and artillery and air.

In summarizing the effects on the enemy, General Seaman said:

(1) A major portion of the enemy's base and control center for operation against the Capital Military District has been destroyed. This represents the loss of an investment of twenty years. The enemy's offensive capability against the Capital Military District has been reduced by loss of personnel, equipment and facilities.
(2) Over 3,700 tons of rice have been captured or destroyed. . . . More significant than the loss itself is the resultant diversion of manpower to reconstitute his stores.
(3) All of the civilian inhabitants of the area, some 6,000 plus their livestock were evacuated. This will deny the enemy food, manpower, revenue, transportation and intelligence.
(4) The capture of over 500,000 separate pages of documents including crypto-material, has given us valuable intelligence. The enemy's security programs have been compromised to include records continuity.
(5) Realization of the seriousness of these losses by the leadership in North Vietnam, COSVN and the VC-dominated populace will have a serious psychological impact.

From every aspect, the enemy had suffered a great defeat. In the words of General Seaman, they would now have to "re-evaluate the relative capabilities of their forces as opposed to ours."

In his analysis of CEDAR FALLS, General Seaman also commented favorably upon another key area, the working relationship between U.S. and South Vietnamese forces:

Cooperation between U.S. and Vietnamese military and civilian agencies was excellent. This was particularly true in the evacuation of the civilian population. Both the ARVN airborne units and the River Assault

Groups provided invaluable assistance in securing and transporting the refugees. Civilian and military personnel of both nations worked in close harmony to organize and build the PHU CUONG refugee camp on very short notice. On the purely military side, ARVN units contributed significantly to the effectiveness of the cordon. The ARVN River Assault Groups made a unique contribution by their patrolling along the river lines.

General DePuy, in his analysis of Operation CEDAR FALLS, stated:

> Operation CEDAR FALLS was long overdue. The Iron Triangle and nearby village of BEN SUC had been lucrative targets for some time. However, this was the first time sufficient forces and equipment were available to properly execute such an undertaking.
>
> The Triangle had been a notorious VC haven. From its confines attacks were launched on the surrounding area, and VC control over such areas was uncontested. Ralliers confirmed that the Triangle contained numerous tunnels and bunkers and huge stores of foodstuffs and equipment. Continual bombing and artillery fires certainly disrupted VC activity, but civilian occupants in the area hampered free-fire activities. Additionally, B-52 strikes and artillery bombardment could not be exploited with ground troops. There were simply no access routes, air or ground, into the heart of the Triangle. The few existing ox cart roads and foot trails were heavily mined and booby trapped. The 100 square kilometers of the Iron Triangle provided a secure jungle haven which no one division could seal, search and destroy.
>
> We had no idea at the beginning that Operation CEDAR FALLS would turn out to be the most significant operation thus far conducted by the 1st Infantry Division. It is most significant in many respects. First of all, it was aimed at the headquarters, Military Region IV. This headquarters is responsible for operations in and around SAIGON. The headquarters directed attacks on TAN SON NHUT and on U.S. troop billets in SAIGON itself.
>
> For the first time in the history of the war in Vietnam, infantry-engineer bulldozer teams cut their way through the jungle, finding and destroying base camps, creating landing zones, pushing back the jungle from roads which can now be used for rapid repenetration of the area. One entire jungle area was completely eliminated. All in all, the engineers cut down 9 square kilometers of solid jungle. This is a technique which will be used again in the penetration of other VC war zones and base areas—a technique pioneered by the 1st Division. Everyone who worked with the engineers recognizes the tremendous contribution they made to the success of the operation.
>
> In addition to the destruction of the base area of Military Region IV, the most significant and unexpected result was the surrender of so many Viet Cong. This has never happened before in the war in Vietnam, and in this area, at least, is a reflection of the complete breakdown in confidence and morale on the part of the VC.
>
> Although I do not expect the war to end quickly, I believe this has been a decisive *turning point* in the III Corps area; a tremendous boost to the morale of the Vietnamese Government and Army; and a blow from which the VC in this area may never recover.

THE RESULTS

In nineteen days, II Field Force, Vietnam, had converted the Iron Triangle from a haven to a sealed battleground and then to a military no-man's-land. Years of work spent tunneling and hoarding supplies were nullified. The civilian population was removed, making any enemy attempt to rebuild doubly difficult. Concealment, particularly along lines of communication, was stripped away, exposing the area to future surveillance. Finally, the area was designated a specified strike zone so that it could be interdicted with ease should the enemy attempt to rebuild. A strategic enemy base had been decisively engaged and destroyed.

By all accounts CEDAR FALLS had to be one of the significant operations in the Vietnam War. Certainly it was *the* significant operation in January 1967; however, that did not mean that there were no operations being conducted in other areas of Vietnam. In fact, in the III Corps Tactical Zone itself there were eighteen separate major military operations conducted during that month, fifteen of them resulting in contact with the enemy.

Intelligence sources summarized the situation in the III Corps area as CEDAR FALLS came to a close as follows, perhaps providing some insight into what the future might have in store:

> During Operation CEDAR FALLS the VC losses in personnel were the equivalent of three battalions. These losses however, were widely scattered and cannot be attributed to specific units. . . . [This defeat] coupled with the recent defeat of [9th VC Division] regiments with resultant loss of major supply stockpiles in the Iron Triangle, Tay Ninh and Phuoc Tuy Provinces indicate the VC will require time for resupply, replacement, retraining, and re-indoctrination. To gain time the VC will, in all probability adapt their Winter Campaign Plan to divert attention from Tay Ninh and other areas selected for reoccupation.

But Generals Westmoreland and Seaman and II Field Force, Vietnam, were not going to give the enemy the time they required or the opportunity to divert attention from the areas in which he had been hit. On the horizon loomed JUNCTION CITY, an operation which was to carry the war deep into enemy sanctuaries in War Zone C for an extended period.

PART TWO

JUNCTION CITY, 22 FEBRUARY–
14 MAY 1967

CHAPTER VIII

Planning and Preparation

JUNCTION CITY was to be the largest operation of the Vietnam war to date and the second one under control of II Field Force, Vietnam. Its primary mission would be search and destroy to eradicate the Central Office of South Vietnam (COSVN) and Viet Cong and North Vietnamese Army installations. Also, various installations such as Special Forces camps and airfields were to be built. Two U.S. divisions, with the commitment of as many as twenty-two U.S. infantry battalions, fourteen artillery battalions, and four South Vietnamese battalions would be involved. JUNCTION CITY would also include the first major combat parachute assault since the Korean War.

Like the Iron Triangle, War Zone C was a major Viet Cong stronghold and had been a sanctuary for insurgents for over twenty years. It was also believed to be the location of headquarters of the Central Office of South Vietnam; however, owing to the remoteness of the area and the strict secrecy with which the enemy treated the headquarters, few facts were known about COSVN installations and units in the area. Clandestine operations conducted in September of 1966 and during Operation ATTLEBORO in November had, however, developed significant intelligence on War Zone C.

In discussing the genesis of Operation JUNCTION CITY, General Seaman, commanding general of II Field Force, Vietnam, stated:

. . . I've got to go back to Operation "Birmingham" which was conducted by the 1st Division in War Zone C, in May of 1966. It was conducted along the Cambodian Border as far north as Lo Go (about 30 kilometers northwest of Tay Ninh City) and the plan was to airlift a brigade into the then suspected location of COSVN headquarters. The 1st Division airlifted one battalion to the area, intending to get an entire brigade there within the day; but, unfortunately, the weather closed in and the rainy season started a couple of weeks earlier than anticipated. So, the decision was made by the division commander, MG DePuy, to withdraw that one battalion, feeling that he could not reinforce it if they got into any difficulty.

Following Operation "Birmingham," General Westmoreland said he wanted me to plan an operation in War Zone C to start as soon as possible after the Christmas and New Year's stand-downs of 1966–1967. He said, in effect, "to think big." This operation was to start about the 8th of January

1967, and would be a multi-division operation including an airborne drop. . . . I (later) briefed General Westmoreland on the progress of our plans for "Junction City" and he approved my concept.

The operation plan, originally named GADSDEN, had three major objectives: to engage the 9th Viet Cong Division and the 101st North Vietnamese Army Regiment; to destroy COSVN headquarters; and to destroy enemy base camps and installations in the area of operation. The plans included a parachute assault by both the 1st Brigade, 101st Airborne Division, and the 173d Airborne Brigade. Among other objectives, the operation was intended to convince the enemy that War Zone C was no longer a haven.

The concept included deception operations prior to the main thrust into War Zone C. During this initial phase, units and supplies would be positioned to support the follow-up effort.

Definitive planning for the operation started in late November 1966. With all intelligence sources of II Field Force, Vietnam, oriented toward collection of information on the operational area, more and more data were received as the starting date for the operation neared. Pattern activity analysis was used extensively, as it had been for CEDAR FALLS; much of the data acquired in that operation was applied in planning JUNCTION CITY. Information on the general location of COSVN and the movements of enemy units of interest was further refined.

From the first planning conference, strict security measures were enforced to prevent compromise. The planning group was held to a minimum within II Field Force, Vietnam, headquarters; whenever possible, preparations were made without specifically identifying them with the operation. However, in December the name of the main operation was changed to JUNCTION CITY because it was believed that the name GADSDEN had been compromised. GADSDEN was shifted to one of the two planned deception operations.

Operation GADSDEN was to be conducted by the U.S. 25th Division in the extreme western portion of War Zone C, in the vicinity of Lo Go. The second preliminary operation, named TUCSON, would be conducted by the U.S. 1st Infantry Division in Binh Long Province, eighty kilometers to the east, in an area generally defined by the Minh Thanh and Michelin rubber plantations and the village of Bau Long on Highway 13. This area also comprised the northern portion of the Long Nguyen secret zone.

Both these preliminary actions were designed as individual division operations in the proximity of the normal division tactical areas of interest. In addition to moving forces for GADSEN and TUCSON, providing a cover for friendly troop buildup on the edges of War Zone C, and establishing supply bases for JUNCTION CITY, it was envisioned that the deception could possibly cause the 271st and 272d Viet Cong Regiments to move into the central area of War Zone C from their then suspected locations.

The plans for JUNCTION CITY, GADSDEN, and TUCSON were published in early December 1966. D-days were set as 3 January for GADSDEN and TUCSON and as 12 January for JUNCTION CITY.

However, as was discussed above, in the middle of December General McChristian, Military Assistance Command J-2, briefed General Seaman on information concerning enemy activities in the Iron Triangle which led to the decision that Operation CEDAR FALLS would be conducted in January. JUNCTION CITY would be postponed until later in February; in turn, GADSDEN was delayed until 2 February and TUCSON postponed until 14 February.

The intelligence concerning War Zone C was continuously being re-examined, and in mid-January the movement and relocation of the 9th Viet Cong Division and the enemy regiments were established. The 271st Regiment was located on the Cambodian border near Lo Go, the 272d Regiment had moved to the Michelin rubber plantation northeast of Dau Tieng, and the 273d was now located outside War Zone C near Tan Uyen, about twenty-five kilometers northeast of Saigon. The 271st and 272d were added as targets for Operations GADSDEN and TUCSON. Headquarters of the 9th Viet Cong Division remained in the eastern sector of War Zone C while intelligence indicated the 101st North Vietnamese Army Regiment—now listed as subordinate to the 9th Division—had moved north to the vicinity of An Loc and Loc Ninh. This new and significant information on the location of enemy units resulted in a shift in the area of primary interest from the eastern to the west central section of War Zone C. The target of major interest became the COSVN headquarters elements.

As D-day for JUNCTION CITY approached, II Field Force intelligence analysts provided these conclusions about the enemy:

> In view of the enemy's recent setbacks in Operation Cedar Falls, and in Tay Ninh Province (ATTLEBORO), the political rejection of the VC by the populace in the national elections (September 1966), and his failure to achieve a major significant victory, the VC will increase guerrilla warfare and terrorism in an effort to wear down and tire the Free World Forces employed in Vietnam. The enemy will use his main forces, when ready, to attack targets that represent significant psychological victories at a minimum risk to his own forces.

The intelligence report listed the following probable enemy courses of action:

1. Intensify guerrilla warfare, acts of terrorism, harassment, propaganda and interdiction of lines of communication.
2. Conduct less than regimental size attacks against isolated forces and installations.
3. Withdraw from main US combat units if he considers the situation unsuitable for a decisive victory.
4. Attack selected targets with forces of regimental strength at a time and place of his own choosing.
5. Continue to secure his base areas and lines of communication.

Events over the next two months would validate these predictions.

The operational area for JUNCTION CITY, War Zone C, is generally defined as the 80x50-kilometer area bounded on the west and north by Cambodia, on the east by Highway 13, and on the south by an east-west line drawn through Ben Cat and Tay Ninh and extending to the Cambodian border. The terrain in the northern and eastern portions rises to approximately one hundred fifty meters while the southern and western portions range in elevation from five to fifty meters. The generally flat, marshy land in the west changes to gently rolling terrain, finally becoming irregular near the eastern province boundary. The predominant land feature in the area is the 987-meter-high Nui Ba Den. Two major rivers drain the area: the Vam Co Dong on the west and the Saigon on the east; neither is fordable. Numerous small streams are found in the eastern portion of War Zone C, the principal ones having steep banks and muddy bottoms.

In the south, trafficability in the area of interest varied from good in the rubber plantations to difficult in marshy areas. In the north, particularly the northeast, movement was difficult because of the heavy forests and dense undergrowth and bamboo but improved in the north and western portions of the province because of the relatively thin forests and scattered open areas.

The ground was expected to be relatively dry during most of the operation. For all practical purposes, at the time JUNCTION CITY was initiated all significant bridges in the operational area had been destroyed, although footbridges had been constructed by the enemy on many of the trails that crisscrossed the area.

At the beginning of JUNCTION CITY the skies over the operational area would be clear, with little precipitation. Later, some rain and cloudiness would occur with patchy early morning fog, limiting visibility in some instances to one mile. The fog generally would dissipate by midmorning. Temperatures would range from a high of 95 to a low of 59 degrees.

Because of the vast area to be covered, the difficult terrain, the enemy anticipated, the number and types of units involved, and the diversity in operations, the planning for JUNCTION CITY was extensive and complex. The mission assigned the planners of II Field Force, Vietnam, read:

    a. Phase I—On order, II FFORCEV in coordination and cooperation with the III ARVN Corps conducts a major offensive into War Zone C (northern Tay Ninh Province) to destroy COSVN and VC/NVA forces and installations.
    b. Phase II—On order, II FFORCEV conducts coordinated airmobile and ground assaults in eastern War Zone C to destroy COSVN and VC/NVA forces and installations.

As originally planned, JUNCTION CITY was to have had only two phases; however, because of the success achieved, Phase III would later be initiated. Its mission: "Continued search and destroy operations north of Highway 247, secure Highway 26 south from Tay Ninh to the junction of Route 239 and secure the towns of Tay Ninh and Suoi Da."

Initially two South Vietnamese regiments were to have participated; however, by January 1967 it was evident that this number was too ambitious and it was reduced to four battalions. In addition, the 1st Brigade of the U.S. 101st Airborne Division was not made available.

As envisioned by II Field Force, preliminary operations GADSDEN and TUCSON, jumping off on 2 and 14 February respectively, would position forces and materiel on the western and eastern extremities of the area of operations. Phase I of JUNCTION CITY would commence on 22 February with five U.S. brigades forming a horseshoe-shaped cordon in the western half of War Zone C. (*Map 8*) The 25th Division would block on the west along the Cambodian border; on the north, along the border, and on the east along Provincial Route 4 would be the 1st Infantry Division with the 173d Brigade attached. On D plus 1 a brigade of the 25th Division and the 11th Armored Cavalry Regiment (attached to the 25th), which had positioned themselves on the southern edge of the horseshoe the previous day, would attack north into the horseshoe. The horseshoe forces would conduct search and destroy operations in their areas. Simultaneous with the detailed and thorough search, a Special Forces and Civilian Irregular Defense Group camp near Prek Klok would be established for future interdiction of enemy supply and infiltration routes in War Zone C. An airstrip capable of handling C–130's would be constructed at the camp. A second similar airfield would be constructed in the vicinity of Katum.

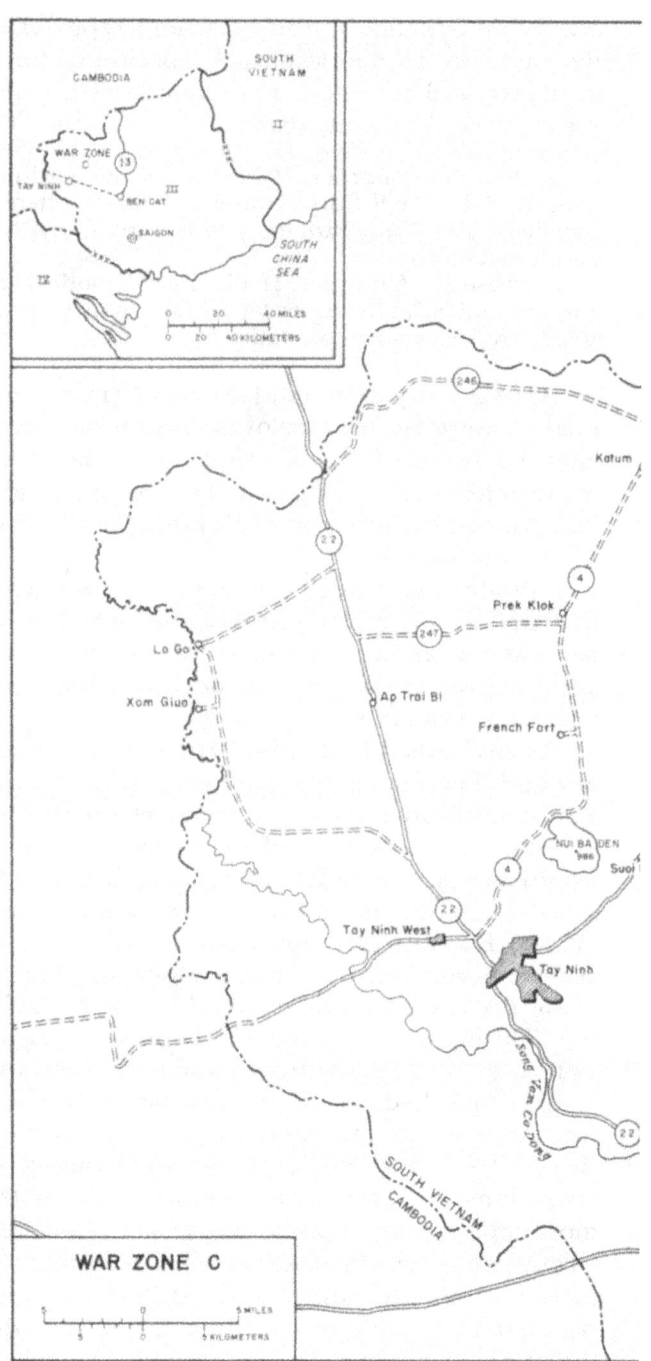

MAP 8

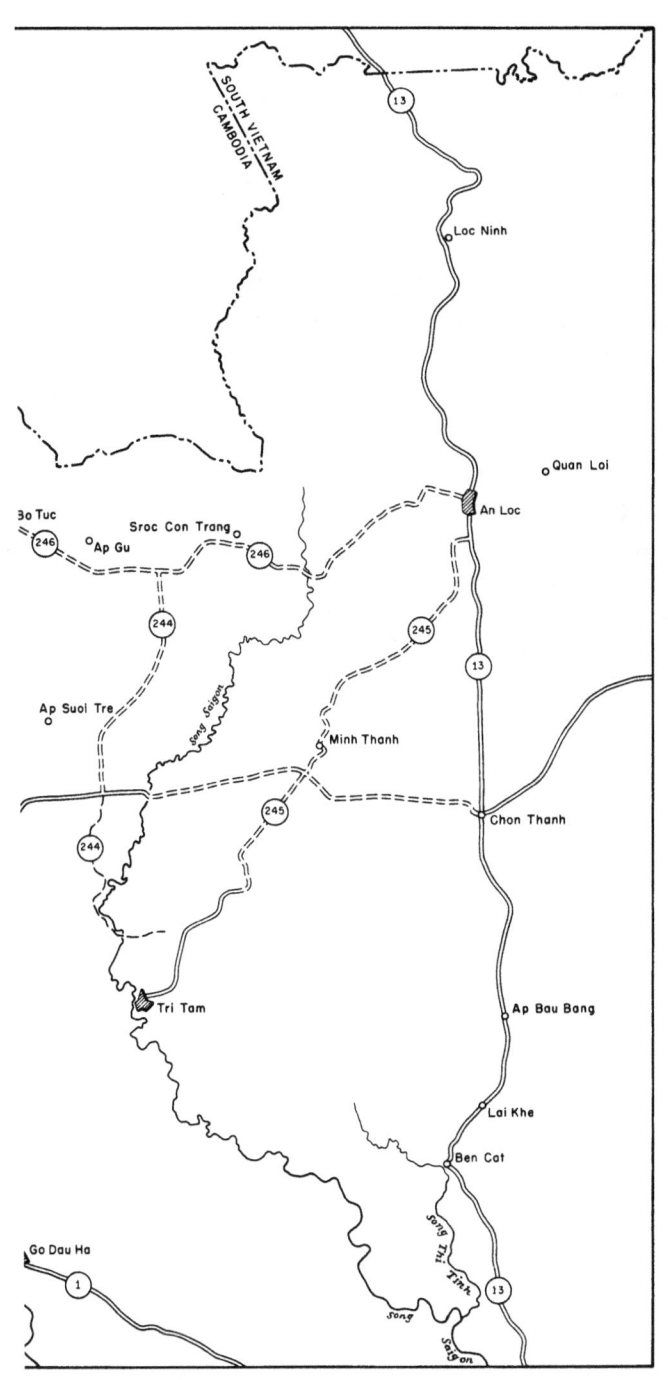

During the operation, particular attention was to be devoted to searching suspected locations of the political and military elements of the Central Office of South Vietnam. A thorough interrogation of all persons apprehended was to be conducted.

During Phase II, II Field Force elements would focus their attention on the eastern portion of War Zone C, conducting search and destroy operations against COSVN, Viet Cong, and North Vietnamese forces and installations. The Saigon River was to be bridged at its intersection with Route 246 west of An Loc. At that site a Special Forces and Civilian Irregular Defense Group camp with an airstrip for C-130's was to be built.

In Phase III, JUNCTION CITY would be reduced to a brigade-size operation in the vicinity of Tay Ninh city in the southern portion of War Zone C. The operational control for this phase would be passed from II Field Force to the 25th Infantry Division.

Operation JUNCTION CITY would demonstrate the ability of American forces to enter areas which had been Viet Cong sanctuaries to conduct successful search and destroy missions and construct facilities in these strongholds. In addition, in the weeks forthcoming each of the four enemy regiments under the 9th Viet Cong Division would be met and defeated.

CHAPTER IX

The Warm-Up Tosses: GADSDEN and TUCSON

Twenty days before the beginning of JUNCTION CITY, preliminary operations were started by the 25th Infantry Division under code name Operation GADSDEN. Twelve days later, on 14 February 1967, the 1st Division's Operation TUCSON jumped off. The primary objective of these operations was the positioning of men and materiel on the western and eastern flanks of the JUNCTION CITY operational area; however, they would become significant in their own right.

Operation Gadsden

Officially classified as a search and destroy operation, GADSDEN employed two brigades of the U.S. 25th Infantry Division under the command of Major General Frederick C. Weyand. Involved were the 3d Brigade, 4th Infantry Division, commanded by Colonel Marshall B. Garth, and the 196th Light Infantry Brigade, Brigadier General Richard T. Knowles commanding.

The GADSDEN area of operation was some thirty kilometers northwest of Tay Ninh, in the vicinity of Lo Go and Xom Giua, South Vietnamese villages on the Cambodian border. (*Map 9*) The terrain is generally flat and the vegetation ranges from rice fields to triple-canopy jungle. During the operation grasslands in the area were as tall as six feet. There was some heavy mud in paddy areas, but most of the previously flooded positions had dried, thus facilitating overland movement. Weather was favorable for the operation.

Before the operation it was suspected that elements of the 271st and 272d Viet Cong Regiments, 70th Guard Regiment, 680th Training Regiment, and miscellaneous elements subordinate to the Central Office of South Vietnam—including several medical units—might be encountered. According to intelligence sources, Lo Go was a major supply center of the Viet Cong forces where shipments from Cambodia were transferred to local units. Therefore, the area of operation was believed to contain extensive supply and ammunition caches, communications storage areas, hospital facilities, base camps, and major training complexes. In addition,

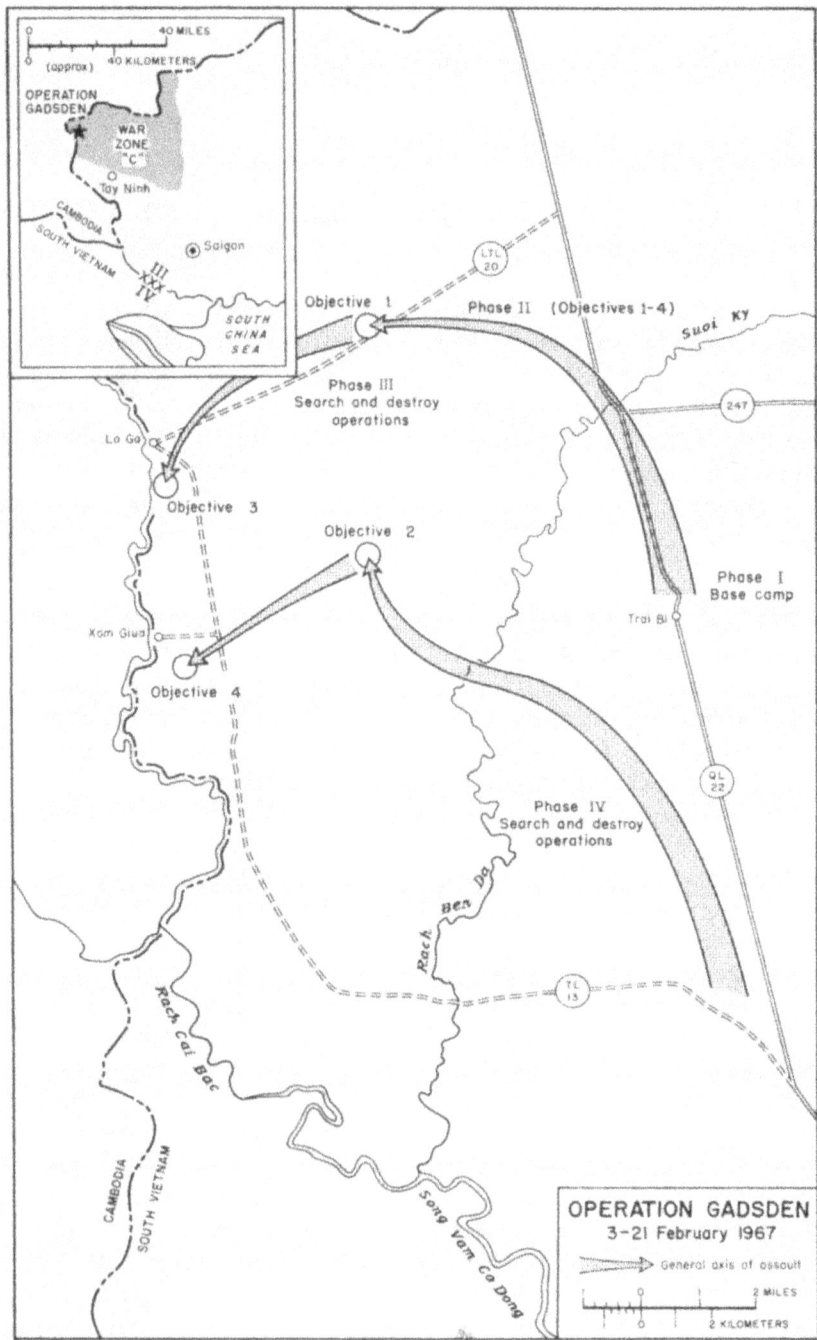

MAP 9

THE WARM-UP TOSSES: GADSDEN AND TUCSON   93

personnel and supply routes to and from Cambodia were expected to be found.

The plans stipulated that Operation GADSDEN be conducted in several phases. During Phase I, forces would be positioned for the attack with combat elements established as close to the operational area as Trai Bi. Phase II, starting on D-day, would include a two-brigade attack to the west to seize two intermediate objectives, secure landing zones, and establish fire support bases. This would be followed by attacks on Lo Go and Xom Giua. Other objectives would be designated later. Search and destroy missions would be conducted in the zone, and blocking positions would be established to seal infiltration and exfiltration routes along the border during Phase III. During the last phase the units would expand the area of operation to the southeast to search for and destroy enemy forces and base camps.

Using a combination of airmobile assaults and attacks by mechanized battalions, the operation went as planned. During the 20-day duration of GADSDEN, the fighting was typified by small unit actions. Even though the fortifications encountered were extensive and many were capable of withstanding very heavy artillery and air strikes, the enemy chose not to stand and fight but rather to employ guerrilla tactics.

Evidence was uncovered to confirm that in the operational area were located a training area for main force Viet Cong units which included an obstacle course and an elaborate land navigation course; a rest and recuperation center including numerous medical facilities and supplies, as well as a 100-gallon still with 2,000 gallons of mash and 50 bottles of alcohol; an ordnance facility for fabricating and storing bombs, artillery rounds, and grenades; and numerous caches of food and other material. Also identified in the area were the postal transportation section, the current affairs section, and the military staff directorate of the Central Office of South Vietnam. Captured documents and ralliers identified elements of the 3d Battalion, 271st Viet Cong Regiment; the 3d Battalion, 70th Viet Cong Regiment; the 680th Training Regiment; and a medical unit subordinate to the Central Office.

In addition to confirming the location of various units and installations in the area, GADSDEN inflicted some fairly significant losses upon the enemy. His casualties totaled at least 161 killed and 2 captured. He lost 26 weapons, 390 tons of rice (of which 50 percent was evacuated), salt, sugar, tea, soap, cigarettes, and 550 pounds of documents. Five hundred fifty huts, 590 bunkers, and 28 sampans were destroyed, as were numerous items of explo-

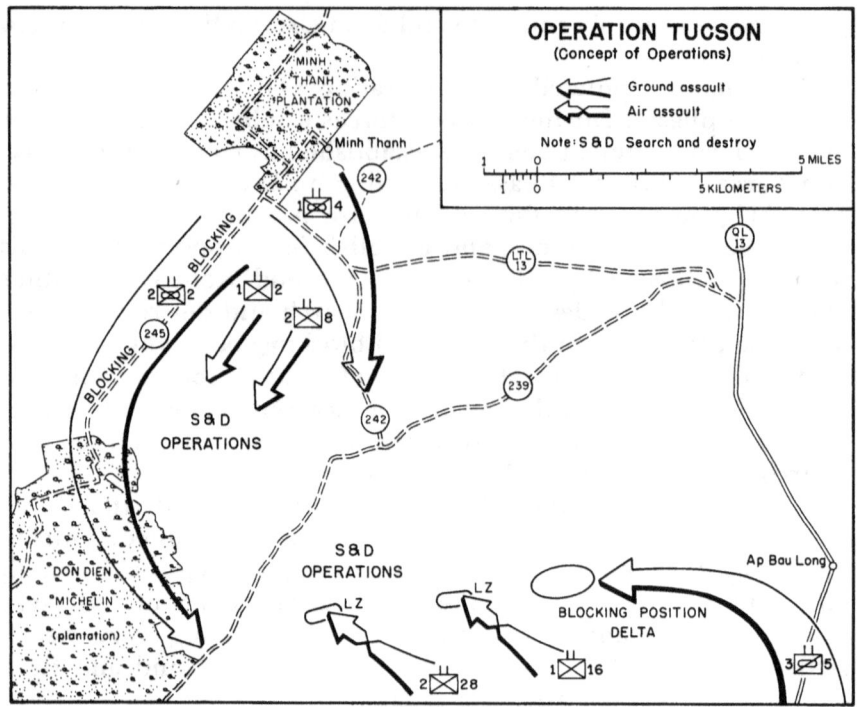

MAP 10

sives and ammunition. U.S. battle losses were 29 killed and 107 wounded.

GADSDEN also accomplished its primary mission of positioning troops and supplies for JUNCTION CITY. The chances of success for that operation were bolstered by the opinion expressed by Colonel Garth: "GADSDEN proved the ability of mechanized units to operate in heavily vegetated terrain and that U.S. forces have the capability of moving at their desire within War Zone C."

Operation Tucson

TUCSON was a 1st Infantry Division operation employing the 1st Brigade under Colonel William B. Caldwell and the 3d Brigade under Colonel Sidney M. Marks. The triangular-shaped area of operations was located in the southwestern corner of Binh Long Province; the town of Minh Thanh was at the north corner, Bau Long on Route 13 at the east corner, and the eastern edge of the Michelin Plantation at the western corner. (*Map 10*) The terrain is gently rolling with the differences in elevation varying less than

INFANTRYMEN MOVE THROUGH HEAVY BRUSH NEAR THE MICHELIN PLANTATION

forty meters. Cross-country movement is generally good along the edges of the area and along the main roads, Routes 239, 242, and 245. The other areas, moderate to dense jungle, are unsuitable for vehicular traffic and poor for foot traffic.

The area was believed to be an enemy sanctuary containing numerous storage sites and base camps. In addition, it was this area, part of the Long Nguyen secret zone, which contained a portion of the "northern rice route," the major logistical and troop channel between War Zones C and D. Enemy units believed to be operating in the area included elements of the 272d Regiment and the Phu Loi Battalion. Other Viet Cong units included the Ben Cat District (local force) Company and one local force platoon from Chon Thanh. Elements of the Binh Long Province and Chon Thanh District Committees were also thought to be in the area.

The plan called for the 1st Brigade to employ a cavalry squadron to attack south from Minh Thanh along Provincial Routes 13 and 242 to secure a position in the center of the operational area. One battalion of mechanized infantry would sweep southwest from Minh Thanh on Route 245 along the edge of the triangular area, taking up blocking positions in a 15-kilometer arc along Route 245 and in the northeastern portion of the Michelin Plantation. Two battalions of infantry would then attack southwest from Minh Thanh between the positions of the cavalry and mechanized forces and conduct search and destroy operations. On the east, under the control of the division's 3d Brigade, a second cavalry squadron (3d of the 5th Regiment of the U.S. 9th Division) would attack north along Route 13 to Bau Long, then turn to the west for eight kilometers, establish a blocking position, and conduct search and destroy operations. Two infantry battalions would make an airmobile assault into landing zones on the southern edge of the operational area between the 3d of the 5th's blocking position and the eastern corner of the Michelin Plantation. From there they would search and destroy. One infantry battalion would be held at Minh Thanh as a Rapid Reaction Force.

The operation was conducted as planned with only sporadic contact with small elements of the enemy. Although captured documents revealed that the 272d Viet Cong Regiment had recently been in the area, only local guards for the caches and base camps were contacted. The period 14–17 February was used for search and destroy operations during which 1,700 tons of rice and 27 tons of salt were found, almost all uncovered by 3d Brigade elements in caches 50 to 200 meters from the trail along which their initial landing zones were located. (This rice would have fed thirteen enemy battalions for one year.)

The enemy lost 13 killed; U.S. casualties were 3 killed and 65 wounded. A few weapons and some small arms ammunition and explosives were found. About 150 installations were destroyed; among them was a regimental-size base camp with four mess halls and a barbed-wire-inclosed cage dug into the ground which appeared to have been a prisoner of war enclosure large enough for about 30 persons.

It was with great disappointment and reluctance that the search and destroy operations came to a close after only four days, since it was obvious that only a fraction of the rice in the area had been discovered. However, it was necessary for the 1st Division to spend the next four days, 18–21 February, completing the primary mission of Tucson, positioning its troops and preparing them for Junction City.

CHAPTER X

Phase I—The Horseshoe Is Pitched

Phase I of Operation JUNCTION CITY was conducted from 22 February to 17 March and involved forces of the U.S. 1st and 25th Infantry Divisions and some South Vietnamese forces deployed in the shape of a giant horseshoe. 1st Division elements constituted the east and north portion of the inverted U; the 25th was assigned the northwestern and western portions and the mission of driving a force north through the open end. With a perimeter of approximately sixty kilometers, the western leg of the horseshoe extended north of Tay Ninh along Route 22 (with major concentration north of Route 247) to the junction at Route 246 on the Cambodian border. The top of the horseshoe was generally delineated by Route 246 (which in that area was nothing more than a cart trail) parallel to the Cambodian border on the north. The east portion continued along Route 246 to the vicinity of Katum and from there south along Route 4 to south of Prek Klok. It was through the southern opening of the horseshoe that 25th Division forces initiated their drive north to conduct search and destroy operations. To the west, south, and east of the horseshoe sweep operations were to be conducted by the units forming it. (*Map 11*)

The controlling headquarters for JUNCTION CITY was II Field Force, Vietnam, under General Seaman. For the first time in the war, II Field Force headquarters displaced to the field and opened a tactical command post at Dau Tieng on D-day.

Combat Forces

During Phase I of Operation JUNCTION CITY the Big Red One, commanded by Major General John H. Hay, Jr., employed two of its three organic brigades (the other remained active on Revolutionary Development operations) and was augmented by the 173d Airborne Brigade and two South Vietnamese units named Task Force WALLACE: the 35th Ranger Battalion and one troop from the 3d Battalion, 1st Cavalry Regiment. Later in Phase I the 1st Brigade, 9th U.S. Infantry Division, joined the 1st Division to keep Route 13 open from Lai Khe to Quan Loi. The division's missions

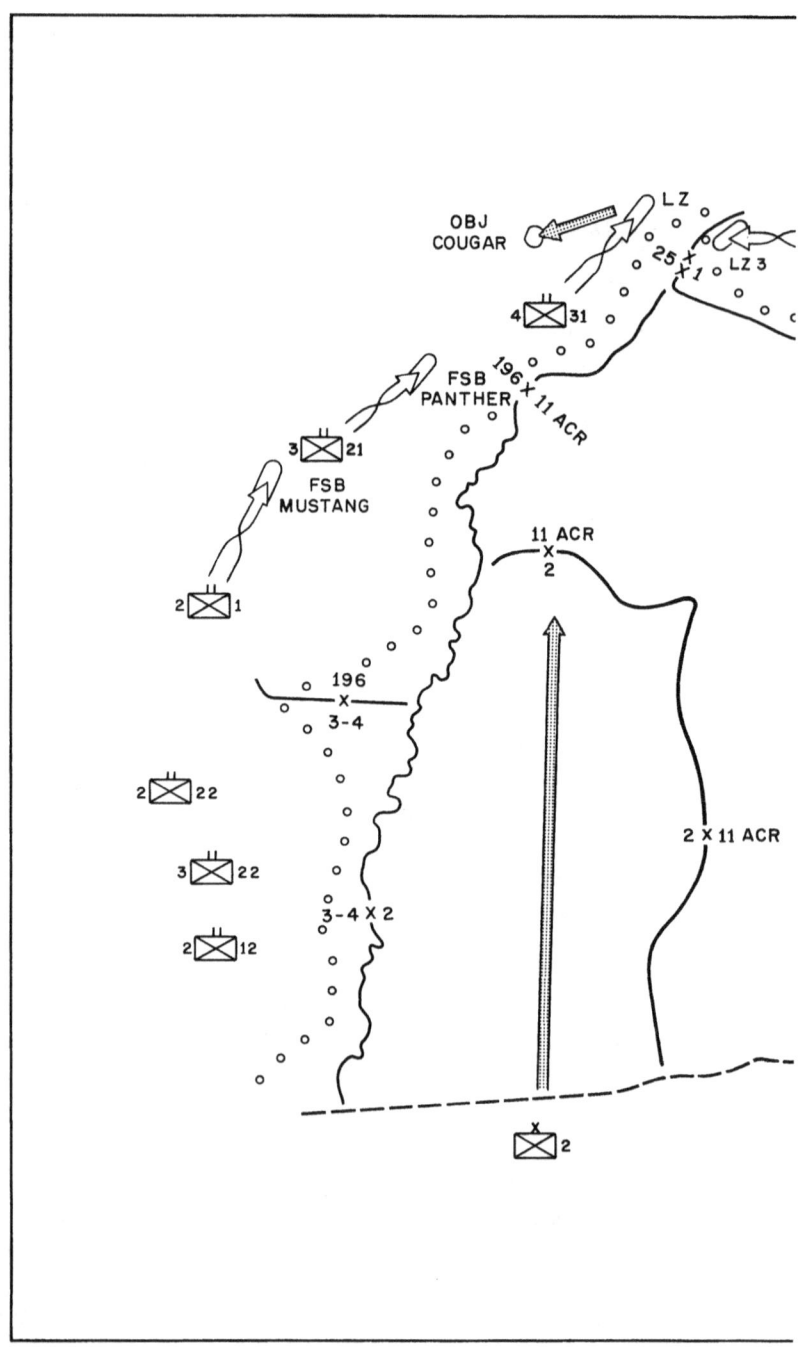

MAP 11

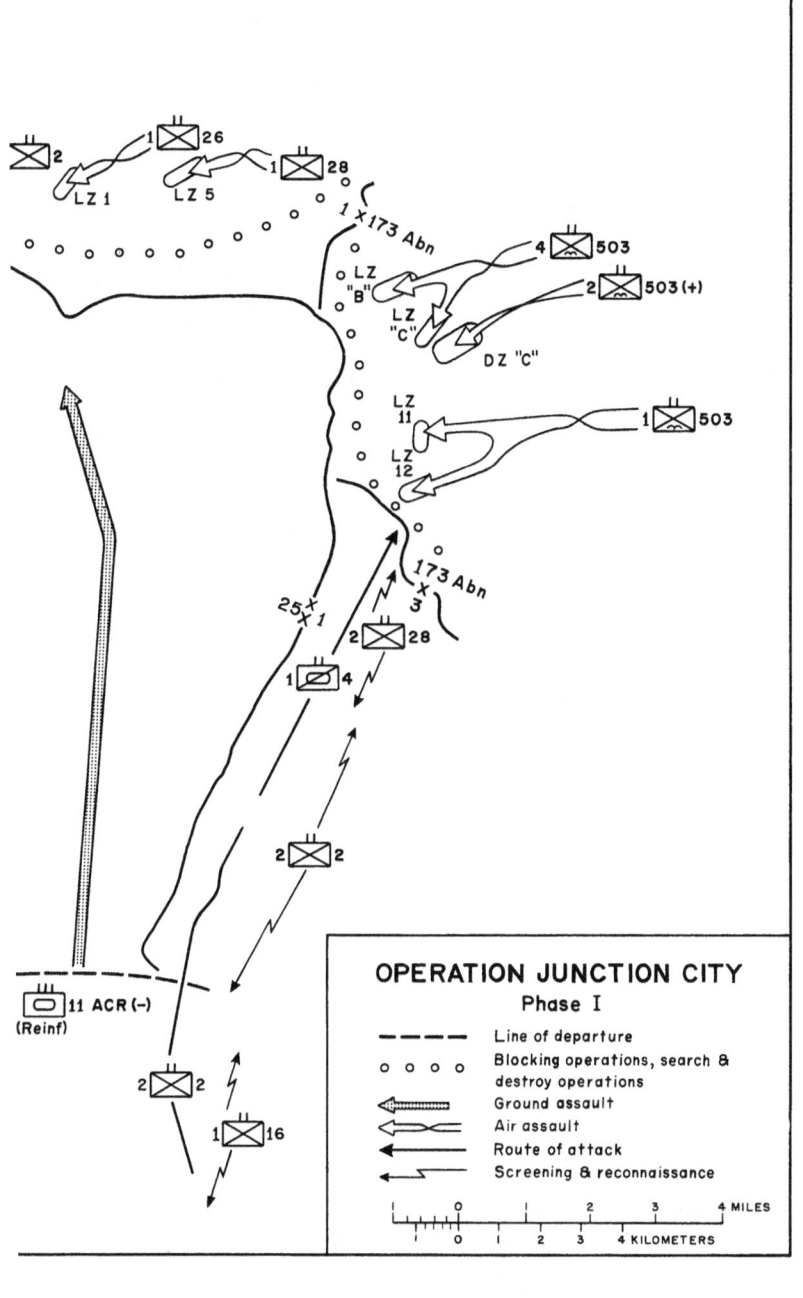

for Phase I were to conduct air and ground assaults to block enemy escape routes in the northern and eastern portion of the area of operations; conduct search and destroy operations; secure lines of communication from Tay Ninh to Katum (consisting of approximately forty-five kilometers of Route 4); and provide security during engineer construction at Katum and Prek Klok. On D-day the 1st Brigade (Colonel Caldwell), comprised of four infantry battalions and Task Force WALLACE, was to assault by air and establish blocking positions in the northern portion of the area. The 173d Airborne Brigade (Brigadier General John R. Deane, Jr.) with three battalions was directed to assault by air on D-day and establish blocking positions from Katum to the 1st Brigade area; this put the 173d on the northeast portion of the horseshoe. Responsibility for the eastern leg of the horseshoe was assigned to the division's 3d Brigade (Colonel Marks). His brigade included one mechanized battalion, an infantry battalion, and the cavalry squadron with one tank company attached. This brigade was to attack north on D-day along Route 4, establish fire support bases, and link up with the 173d. Each of the brigades had at least one artillery battalion in direct support.

During Phase I of Operation JUNCTION CITY, the 25th (Tropic Lightning) Division under General Weyand employed its organic 2d Brigade with other units under division control, namely, the 3d Brigade, 4th Infantry Division; 196th Light Infantry Brigade; 11th Armored Cavalry Regiment (–); and two South Vietnamese units, the 1st and 5th Marine Battalions (Task Force ALPHA). The 1st Brigade, 9th Infantry Division, part of the division's task organization, was placed under the operational control of the 1st Infantry Division later in Phase I.

Under the 25th Division's plan, the 3d Brigade, 4th Infantry Division (Colonel Garth), would block and continue to conduct search and destroy operations from the area which it held at the close of Operation GADSDEN on 21 February in the far western portion of the operational area. Assigned to the brigade were one mechanized infantry battalion, two infantry battalions, one troop of cavalry, and a company of armor. Operating closely with Garth's brigade was the 196th Brigade (General Knowles), which on D-day would conduct airmobile assaults with its three infantry battalions along the northwest portion of the horseshoe to establish blocking positions and seal enemy escape routes into Cambodia. The positions of the 25th Division units would thus form the broad left leg of the horseshoe and would complete, along with the 1st Division, the seal of the operational area. The division's 2d Brigade (Colonel Marvin D. Fuller) and Colonel William W. Cobb's 11th Armored

PHASE I—THE HORSESHOE IS PITCHED 101

Cavalry Regiment (−) constituted the hammer forces that on D plus 1 would drive north into the horseshoe to locate and destroy enemy forces and facilities.

Both the Tropic Lightning Division and the Big Red One started deploying forces for JUNCTION CITY on 18 February (D minus 4) and were ready to roll by D-day.

D-Day, 22 February 1967

On D-day the operation order was implemented as envisaged. Nine infantry battalions conducted air assaults (eight airmobile, one parachute) to cordon the entire northern portion of the objective area. At the same time, the 25th Division adjusted its one brigade in blocking positions on the west while positioning additional units for the attack into the horseshoe; the 3d Brigade, 1st Division, pushed north up Provincial Route 4 to complete the horseshoe.

The 1st Brigade, 1st Division, initiated the airmobile operations from Minh Thanh with one battalion making an airmobile assault at 0813 into a landing zone north of Route 246 and only 1,600 meters south of the Cambodian border. Sporadic small arms fire was encountered from the southern portion of the landing zone; however, the zone was quickly secured. The other two battalions of the brigade air assaulted into LZ's to the west of the first battalion at 1130 and 1630. They were unopposed.

Earlier that day, 845 paratroopers had boarded sixteen C–130's at Bien Hoa and at 0900 the 173d Airborne Brigade began its combat jump. As the aircraft approached the drop zone (three kilometers north of Katum), the jumpmaster's voice rose above the roar of the C–130: "Stand in the Door." General Deane moved to the right door; taking his position in the left door was Lieutenant Colonel Robert H. Sigholtz, commander of the airborne task force composed of the 2d Battalion, 503d Infantry; A Battery, 3d Battalion, 319th Artillery; and elements of the 173d Brigade headquarters and headquarters company. As the green light flashed "go," General Deane jumped, leading the first U.S. combat parachute assault since the Korean War. There was no enemy contact during the jump.

(Chief Warrant Officer Howard P. Melvin of San Francisco, California, then 53 years old, was participating in his fifth combat parachute assault over a period of some twenty years. His previous four were Gela, Sicily, Salerno, and St. Mere Eglise.)

By 0920 all companies had established command posts. A heavy equipment drop commenced at 0925 and continued periodically

Individual Ammunition Issue

throughout the day. By 1230 the battalion command post was established. There had been only eleven minor injuries as a result of the jump.

Almost simultaneously with the airborne assault, the 196th Brigade of the 25th Division began airmobile assaults in the vicinity of Route 246 along the northwestern portion of the horseshoe. By 1350 all three battalions had completed their assaults unopposed.

The northeastern portion of the inverted U was completed by the two other battalions of the 173d Brigade, then at Quan Loi, making their airmobile assaults into four landing zones, three north and one south of Katum.

Ground elements for the operation had started rolling at 0630 on D-day as the 1st Division's 3d Brigade entered the action. While an infantry battalion remained in Suoi Da, other forces of the brigade attacked north along Route 4 from Artillery Base I at the "French Fort." Following the attacking force, the mechanized infantry battalion moved into defensive positions at planned artillery bases near Prek Klok and three kilometers to the north.

Artillery for the bases was in the column and was dropped off as the column came to the appropriate fire base. In the column was also the armored company of the 173d Brigade which would revert to the brigade's control upon linkup. Although there were temporary delays in getting the column pushed through caused by mines, road repair, and the need to bridge some streams, the linkup with elements of the 173d just south of Katum occurred at 1500.[1] The division engineer elements in the column had had a busy day in making Route 4 passable and in launching three AVLB's over streams.

The 2d Brigade, 25th Division, and the 11th Armored Cavalry Regiment (-) moved to positions near the open (south) end of the horseshoe and poised for their attack to the north in the morning. The remaining brigade under the 25th Division continued search and destroy operations east of Route 22 and north of Trai Bi.

Eighteen battalions, organized into six brigades, and one cavalry regiment were now deployed around the horseshoe. Thirteen mutually supporting fire support bases also ringed the operational area.

Throughout the day enemy contact and casualties remained light with four Americans killed and twenty-three wounded; enemy losses were unknown. The Air Force had also had a busy day, having flown 216 preplanned strike sorties in direct support of the ground operation.

D Plus 1, 23 February

The combined elements of the 11th Armored Cavalry Regiment (-) and the 2d Brigade of the 25th Division thrust northward through the open end of the horseshoe to trap the Viet Cong and locate and destroy COSVN and North Vietnamese Army–Viet Cong installations. The units immediately began to uncover significant caches of enemy supplies and equipment. Only four minor contacts, however, were made during the day's search.

Around the horseshoe the units continued to improve their defensive positions, to secure routes in their areas, and to conduct search and destroy operations. Contact remained light. One sig-

---

[1] When I landed at the 173d Brigade command post in late morning to make final coordination for the linkup of the 3d Brigade column, I was interested to observe both the sense of euphoria and the lassitude which obviously had enveloped many of the jumpers I saw. The former feeling, I understand, resulted from the jump having been most successful; the latter, I suspect, came as the aftermath to the severe jolt of adrenalin most of the jumpers must have received as they contemplated their first jump in months being made into a potentially "hot" drop zone located only four kilometers from the Cambodian border. Small wonder their glands were functioning!

ELEMENTS OF THE 11TH ARMORED CAVALRY REGIMENT *guarding road to rubber plantation, 23 February 1967.*

nificant find in the 1st Brigade, 1st Division, area was a battalion-size base camp complete with shower facilities and over 6,000 pairs of "Ho Chi Minh" sandals (made from worn-out truck tires). The infantry battalion of the 3d Brigade, 1st Division, which had remained at Suoi Da, air assaulted into a landing zone near Route 4, three kilometers southwest of Katum. Another infantry battalion from Minh Thanh replaced it at Suoi Da. Task Force ALPHA consisting of the 1st and 5th South Vietnamese Marine Battalions was airlifted from Saigon to Trai Bi and was attached to the 25th Division. Engineers continued to improve Route 4 and started the construction of a timber trestle bridge about four kilometers south of Katum. Tactical air strikes for the day numbered 175.

D Plus 2, 24 February

General Seaman sent a message to the commanding generals of the 1st and 25th Divisions congratulating them on the speed

PHASE I—THE HORSESHOE IS PITCHED

Moving Through the Jungle

and professionalism displayed during the placement of the cordon in western War Zone C. He concluded by saying ". . . I want a thorough search to be made of areas of responsibility. . . . I particularly desire that western War Zone C be completely covered." Just as a similar one sent in CEDAR FALLS had done, General Seaman's message was to set the tone for JUNCTION CITY for the next twenty-one days.

On 24 February Task Force ALPHA conducted an airmobile assault into a landing zone secured by the 196th Brigade at the northern end of its area of responsibility near the Cambodian border; the South Vietnamesee marines attacked south within the zone and prepared to continue operations farther to the south. The infantry battalion of the 3d Brigade, 1st Division, which was at Suoi Da, moved to field positions six kilometers south of Prek Klok along Route 4.

The hammer forces of the 25th Division continued the attack to the north. The other II Field Force units on the horseshoe strengthened further their defensive blocking positions and continued search and destroy operations. The engineers continued to improve the road network and started to clear the jungle up to seventy-five yards from the sides of Route 4. Construction of the airfield at Katum also commenced.

Resistance was light and scattered throughout the day and into the night; however, six enemy base camps were located and destroyed. The bases contained a significant number of weapons, ammunition, rice, and miscellaneous supplies of all types, "from fish-sauce to dynamite." It was on this day that a series of base camps in an area three kilometers south of the Cambodian border began to be uncovered by one of the battalions of the 1st Brigade, 1st Division; and they had to fight their way in. It appeared that the camps were part of the military affairs section of the Central Office of South Vietnam. There were large mess facilities, lecture halls, recreational areas, and supply depots. Among some of the unusual items found in them were over 30 excellent portable transistor radios made in Japan, over 4,500 batteries for such radios, reams of paper, 700 pencils, 500 ball-point pens, 1,750 erasers, a new Briggs and Stratton 3-hp. engine and generator, shower points, and ping-pong tables. A visit to one of these base camps revealed large underground living quarters and big, heavily built defensive positions. Above ground were some sleeping quarters and cooking areas with roofs made of leaves so they could not be seen through the jungle canopy. In one of these cooking facilities was a calendar pad nailed to a roof support. The date exposed was 23 February, the day U.S. forces first entered the general area of the base camps. The occupants had departed in a hurry, leaving behind food partially prepared in the kitchens as well as their livestock and chickens.

By the end of the third day of the operation, all was still going according to plan. Forty-two of the enemy had been killed and 1 prisoner and 4 ralliers taken; U.S. losses were 14 killed and 93 wounded.

End of Phase I, 25 February–17 March

During the rest of Phase I (which was officially terminated at midnight of 17 March) the units of both divisions continued their meticulous search of the operational area. Since the hammer forces had completed their operations, the units of the 1st Brigade, 1st Division, started leaving their portion of the horseshoe as early as 2 March when one battalion was airlifted to Quan Loi. A second battalion was lifted the following day to Minh Thanh, and on 4

HACKING OUT A TRAIL

March the 1st Brigade terminated Phase I. On 3 March the 1st Engineers completed the Katum airfield;[2] the next day all of the battalion had terminated Phase I and began relocating to the eastern edge of War Zone C. (For all intents and purposes the 1st Brigade of the 1st Division and the 1st Engineer Battalion began Phase II on 7 March when they started operations west of An Loc along Route 246 and at the destroyed bridge site where that road crosses the Saigon River.)

During this 21-day period the action was marked mainly by contacts with small forces (one to ten men) and the continual discovery of more and more base camps. Rice, documents, dried fish,

---

[2] On 22 February, after twenty-seven days of labor, D Company of the 1st Engineers had just finished the construction of a C–130 capable airfield (covered with T17 membrane) at Suoi Da. Two days later the company was at Katum starting work on another airfield. Within eight days they cleared 680,000 square feet of jungle; opened a laterite pit; and graded, crowned, drained, compacted, and completed the laterite airfield. On 3 March Air Force Colonels V. W. Froelich of the 315th Air Command Wing and Hugh Wild, 834th Air Division, flew in by transport and inspected and approved the field. They hauled out a load of captured rice.

Company Sweep in War Zone

ammunition and explosives, some weapons, and much communication equipment (including miles of wire) were the principal items found. Along Route 4 convoy vehicles continued to hit mines and be harassed by RPG2 antitank weapons and small arms fire.

The two major battles fought during Phase I occurred at or near Prek Klok on 28 February and 10 March. However, there were other occurrences and sizable engagements during this period which are worthy of mention.

On 26 February a company of the 3d Brigade, 4th Division, west of Route 22, engaged the 3d Battalion, 271st Viet Cong Regiment, in the latter's base camp. The company was completely surrounded and another company came to its relief. Eleven enemy were killed with U.S. losses 5 killed and 19 wounded.

Two days later the 173d Brigade northeast of Katum found what appeared to be the public information office for psychological propaganda of the Central Office of South Vietnam. In an underground photographic laboratory the troopers found 120 reels of motion picture film, numerous still photographs, and pictures and

PHASE I—THE HORSESHOE IS PITCHED

AN INFANTRYMAN RETURNS FIRE DURING AN ENEMY ATTACK

busts of Communist leaders. This discovery proved to be one of the major intelligence coups of the war.

On the following day, 1 March, a battalion of the 1st Brigade, 1st Division, sweeping in the same general area as the location of the COSVN military affairs section, found what appeared to be a school and propaganda center. There were light, office-type huts, a mess hall, two dispensaries, and sleeping quarters, but no fighting positions. Among the items taken were a loudspeaker system complete with speakers and amplifiers, material for making identification cards, and a bag of documents.

On 3 March a company of the 173d Brigade made contact with an estimated enemy company east of Katum. In an intensive fire fight in which the enemy used small arms, automatic weapons, and M79 grenade launchers, and which lasted only thirty minutes, the enemy lost 39 killed and the U.S. 20 killed and 28 wounded.

On 6 March the 173d Brigade made airmobile assaults with its three battalions into three landing zones located one, three, and six kilometers south of Bo Tuc (on Route 246 southeast of Katum).

The brigade was searching for the COSVN military intelligence bureau reported to be located south of Bo Tuc. During the next seven days of search and destroy the battalions made sporadic contact, killing about 40 Viet Cong.

Having completed its participation in the hammer operation, the 11th Armored Cavalry Regiment (−) had tuned west on 26 February to continue search and destroy in the 25th Division's operational area. On 6 March the two squadrons of the 11th Armored Cavalry began a sweep along the Cambodian border. The sweep was to cover a zone extending 1,500 meters from the border and was to start four kilometers southwest of the point where Route 22 hits the Cambodian border in the north and was to end at Lo Go. The sweep would include all the border in the "Little Elephant's Ear" proper. Just after noon on 11 March one troop was brought under small arms, automatic weapons, RPG2, and recoilless rifle fire from an estimated Viet Cong company at six kilometers northwest of Lo Go and within 200 meters of the Cambodian border. The enemy was in well-prepared positions with fortified bunkers and an extensive trench system. As friendly fires and air strikes increased, the Viet Cong were trapped on the near bank of the river which marks the border at this point; helicopter gunships kept the river under surveillance to prevent escape into Cambodia. During the night the position was kept under continuous illumination by flareships and under artillery and minigun fire from the flareships. However, the enemy slipped away during the night, leaving twenty-eight dead behind. The reason for the stiff resistance became readily apparent the next morning. Located in reinforced concrete bunkers fifteen feet underground were two large, electrically powered Chinese printing presses weighing nearly a ton each. Manufactured in Shanghai in 1965, each press had an hourly output of 5,000 printed sheets measuring 17 by 24 inches; the presses also had cutting and folding attachments. A further search yielded several barrels of lead printer's type as well as thirty-one individual weapons. The presses were airlifted to the 25th Division's base camp. Indications were that the presses were being utilized by the COSVN propaganda and cultural indoctrination section.

The Phase I operations started to wind down beginning 12 March. On the 14th the 3d Brigade, 1st Division, turned over responsibility for the security of Prek Klok Special Forces Camp, the old French Fort, and Route 4 to the 196th Brigade. Colonel Marks commenced repositioning his forces and prepared to relieve the division's 2d Brigade of its Revolutionary Development mission so the brigade could participate in JUNCTION CITY II. On 15 March the 173d left the operational area and reverted to control of II Field Force; on the same day the 11th Cavalry (−) terminated its participation. At midnight on 17 March Phase I officially came to a close. The enemy had lost 835 killed, 15 captured, 264 weapons, and enormous quantities of supplies and equipment.

CHAPTER XI

The Battles of Prek Klok

Prek Klok I

The 1st Battalion, 16th Infantry, had become a part of JUNCTION CITY on D plus 1 (23 February) when it was airlifted from its base camp at Lai Khe to Suoi Da. There it assumed the mission which had belonged to the 2d Battalion, 28th Infantry, of being the reserve for the 3d Brigade; it also was assigned its portion of the Suoi Da defenses. In the early morning hours of 24 February the 1st Battalion area received approximately one hundred twenty rounds of 82-mm. mortar, all within a few minutes; two were killed (including a company commander) and five wounded. Six hours later the battalion was airlifted to positions along Route 4 north of Suoi Da and, after considerable jungle clearing, went into a night defensive position on the east side of Route 4, six kilometers south of Prek Klok. (At Prek Klok was an artillery base defended by the 2nd Battalion, 2d Infantry [-]; the initial engineer activities leading to the construction of a Special Forces and Civilian Irregular Defense Group camp and airstrip were also under way.) The mission of the 1st of the 16th was to secure the road in its assigned sector and to engage in search and destroy operations.

The 1st of the 16th was under the command of Lieutenant Colonel Rufus C. Lazzell. This was the second time in less than a year that he had commanded "the Rangers." In mid-1966 he had been the commanding officer for about a month until he was wounded by a .50-caliber round in the battle of Minh Thanh Road on 9 July. The wound to his elbow was serious enough for him to be evacuated to the United States; upon his return to the division in November 1966, General DePuy gave him back his old command.

On 25 February Colonel Lazzell must have thought his outfit was hexed. First had been the mortaring at Suoi Da. This was followed on the 25th by one of his battalion's 81-mm. mortar rounds falling short and injuring two of his men. On the same day his position caught some .50-caliber machine gun rounds from a friendly mechanized unit conducting reconnaissance by fire during

THE BATTLES OF PREK KLOK

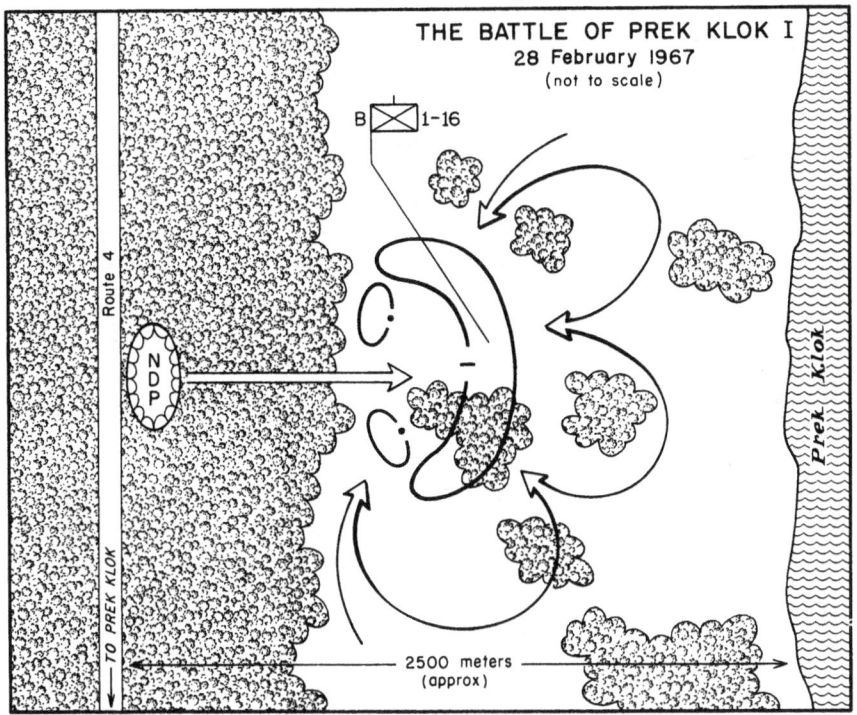

MAP 12

the early hours of darkness. The only damage was to an 81-mm. mortar. The next two days went fairly smoothly for "Rufe's Rangers," but the 28th would be a busy day for them.

What follows is the story of the first battle of Prek Klok and is in part drawn from an account carried in the December 1967 issue of the Big Red One's magazine in Vietnam, *Danger Forward*. It is also based upon other references and upon the recollections of some of us who were there. (*Map 12*)

At 0800 on 28 February, Company B of the 1st Battalion, 16th Infantry, left the battalion's night defensive position located along Route 4 and proceeded east on a search and destroy mission. Twenty-five hundred meters to the front was the stream named Prek Klok; they would never reach it.

The extremely slow movement through the thick and tangled jungle was made in two columns with the 3d Platoon in the lead, followed by the 2d and 1st Platoons. Captain Donald S. Ulm (who would later receive the Silver Star for his part in the action) commanded the company; he and his command element were located between the 2d and 1st Platoons.

As the company pushed on, the jungle thinned somewhat and the primary obstacle to the infantrymen became the fallen trees and brush—deadfall—which was encountered at 50- to 75-meter intervals. The company employed patrols in a cloverleaf pattern as the unit moved forward. Two such patterns had been completed by the time Company B progressed a little over one kilometer from its starting point that morning.

At 1030 the lead element of the 3d Platoon received small arms and automatic weapons fire from its front. The enemy force was initially thought to be and reported a company-size unit, but when Captain Ulm learned that three enemy machine guns had been observed, he correctly concluded that the enemy force was considerably larger. The enemy was well concealed, but not dug in and thus not fully prepared for the fight to follow. It was a meeting engagement of the two forces.

The 3d Platoon, still in the lead, continued to receive heavy fire and was unable to gain fire superiority. Then the platoon reported being attacked on its right (south) flank as well as from its front to the east.

As was the policy within the division for most operations of this nature, artillery marching fire had been preceding the company as it moved east; it was being fired by the 2d Battalion, 33d Artillery (105-mm.), located at Artillery Base II at Prek Klok. As soon as contact was made the artillery forward observer called for a shift of fires to the enemy's location. Within minutes one of the command and control Huey helicopters of the division was over the point of contact and in touch with both the division tactical operations center and, in the absence of the brigade and battalion commanders, the company on the ground. The tactical operations center was alerted to get a forward air controller airborne over the area and to be prepared to get air strikes into the area at the rate of one each fifteen minutes. Since the enemy was not dug in, the ordnance requested was CBU (cluster bomb units), which are delivered almost at treetop level with a bursting radius of thirty meters. They could be delivered very close to friendly units and were a highly lethal weapon against enemy troops in the open, even in the jungle; it was the ordnance preferred by the Big Red One for these conditions.

Captain Ulm was requested to mark the position of his troops on the ground with colored smoke and to give, as best he could, the disposition of his company with respect to the smoke. It was quickly apparent to the airborne observer that the artillery (now supported by a battery of 155-mm. howitzers at Artillery Base I—

the French Fort to the south) had to be shifted if it were to be effective. The shift was made.

Twenty minutes after the initial contact, the enemy launched an attack from the northeast. Contact was lost between the 3d Platoon and the command group. Captain Ulm theorized that the 3d Platoon and possibly the 2d Platoon would be flanked from the direction of the renewed attack and directed the 1st Platoon to move to the left flank of the 3d Platoon. As the men moved into position the entire company area was hit by small arms fire, rifle grenades, rockets, and 60-mm. mortar rounds. The firing was intense, but it resulted in few friendly casualties. The 2d Platoon moved to the right.

At 1230 radio contact was re-established with the 3d Platoon. Captain Ulm learned that the company was in an arc-shaped formation with the 3d Platoon in the center, 2d on the right, and 1st on the left (north). From this information the airborne observer was better able to picture the disposition on the ground and adjust the artillery and air strikes accordingly. As each flight arrived over the target and its ordnance was determined, Captain Ulm was asked where he wanted it placed. Each time, a colored smoke grenade was thrown by the unit on the ground, and the strike was brought in with relation to the smoke as desired.

Captain Ulm noted that much of the automatic weapons and small arms fire was coming from the trees and that the fire was extremely accurate. The company's efforts were now directed at the expertly camouflaged and well concealed snipers in the trees.

At approximately 1300 the 2d Platoon detected movement to the west, and it appeared that the enemy was attempting to encircle the company and attack the open (west) end of the perimeter. To meet this threat, a fire team from the 1st Platoon was moved to the northwest and a squad from the 2d Platoon was moved to the southwest. As the squad from the 2d Platoon moved into position, it received heavy automatic weapons fire from the trees. The fire was returned and artillery fire was called in on the western side of the company.

Air strikes continued to be placed as directed by the commander on the ground. In more than one instance the word came to the forward air controller: "Drop it within thirty yards of the smoke." The artillery was also being brought in as close as was dared. By 1400 the battle had subsided into sniper fire, and by 1500 contact was broken. Credit had to go to the fifty-four sorties of the Tactical Air Command and the intensive artillery fire.

In the meantime Colonel Marks, the brigade commander, at

1430 brought another company of the 1st Battalion, 16th Infantry, into a landing zone some six hundred meters to the northeast of the point of contact following the firing of preparatory fires around the zone. Upon landing one man was wounded by small arms fire. A second company from another battalion securing Minh Thanh was lifted into the landing zone immediately after the first had secured it; this second company was dispatched to assist Captain Ulm's unit. By 1645 a third company, also from the 1st Battalion, landed to assist in securing the landing zone and in evacuating the dead and wounded who would be brought to it.

It was not until 2130 that Captain Ulm and his company, assisted by the relieving company, reached the landing zone with their 25 dead and 28 wounded. It had been a long day. A sweep of the area of contact by the relieving company that evening and another sweep the following morning revealed 167 enemy dead and 40 enemy weapons captured or destroyed. A prisoner captured in the battle area the morning after turned out to be the assistant commander of a company in the 2d Battalion, 101st North Vietnamese Army Regiment of the 9th Viet Cong Division. It was his battalion which had met Company B. It appeared that meeting engagement with Captain Ulm and company prevented the North Vietnamese battalion from reaching Route 4 and attacking one of the many U.S. convoys traveling between Suoi Da and Katum.

The morning after the fight was one of those beautiful mornings typical of that time of year. An officer walking among the survivors in the landing zone and chatting with them asked one of the young soldiers: "What did you think of the artillery and the air strikes—were they coming in a little close?" The soldier turned on a big grin and replied: "Sir, I was getting sprayed all over. But God it felt good!"

In speaking to the assembled company before they choppered out of the landing zone later than morning, this same officer said:

> Although many of your leaders were wounded, the company never lost control of the situation. The NCO's and enlisted men performed like the truly magnificent soldiers they are. . . . The medevac (medical evacuation) effort was outstanding. Considering the dense jungle in which they were working, the medical personnel, both on the ground and in the air, were professionals from beginning to end.

With that, Company B loaded onto choppers and headed for Suoi Da to be refitted and receive replacements. Five days later they were back in action.

Among those persons who more than qualified for accolades on that day, none was more deserving than Platoon Sergeant

FIRST LIEUTENANT EDWARD CHRISTIANSEN, COMPANY A, 1ST BATTALION, 16TH INFANTRY, *calls for air strikes over a suspected Viet Cong position.*

Matthew Leonard of Birmingham, Alabama. When his platoon leader was wounded during the initial contact, Sergeant Leonard organized the platoon defensive position, redistributed ammunition, and inspired his men. While dragging a wounded soldier to safety a sniper's bullet shattered his hand, but he refused medical attention and continued to fight. Under cover of the main attack from the northeast, the enemy moved a machine gun into a location where it could sweep the entire position of Sergeant Leonard's platoon. Sergeant Leonard rose to his feet, charged the gun, and destroyed its crew despite being hit several times by enemy fire. When last seen alive, he was propped against a tree continuing to engage the enemy. Sergeant Leonard was awarded the Medal of Honor posthumously.

Prek Klok II

The second major battle of Operation JUNCTION CITY took place on 10 March. The following description of that battle is also based

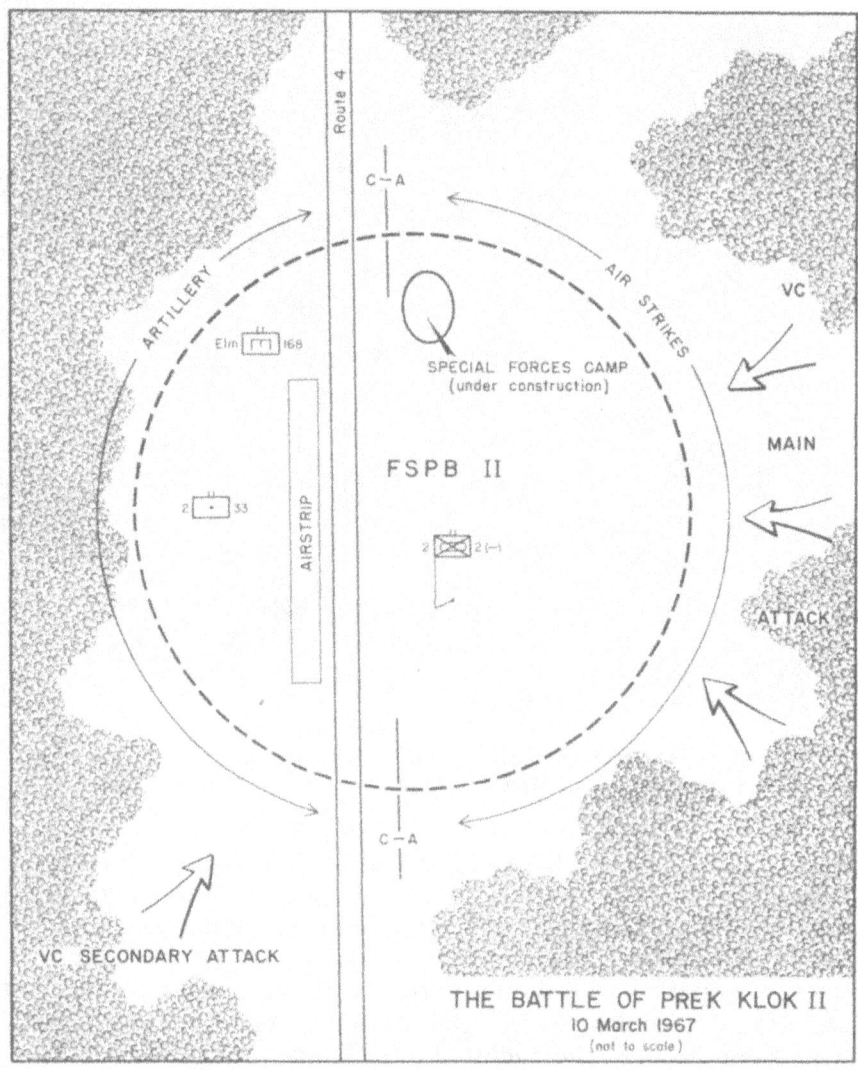

MAP 13

in part upon the account presented in the December 1967 edition of *Danger Forward*.

On the evening of the 10th, the 2d Battalion (Mechanized), 2d Infantry (minus Company B), commanded by Lieutenant Colonel Edward J. Collins, was securing the perimeter of Artillery Fire Support Patrol Base II located at Prek Klok on Route 4, twenty kilometers north of Nui Ba Den. (*Map 13*) Inside the circular "wagon train" perimeter of the base were headquarters, B and C

Batteries of the 2d Battalion, 33d Artillery (Lieutenant Colonel Charles D. Daniel), plus elements of the 168th Engineer Battalion. The engineers were busily engaged in building a Special Forces and Civilian Irregular Defense Group camp and airstrip.

The 2d Battalion's APC's (armored personnel carriers) were placed at 50-meter intervals around the base perimeter. The areas between the tracks were protected by foxholes manned by infantrymen, engineers, and artillerymen.

Just after dusk fell, the troops on the perimeter fired a "mad minute" to test their weapons and provide a show of force to the enemy. Ambush patrols and listening posts left the perimeter for their positions in the surrounding jungle. At about 2030, men of an A Company listening post to the east of the perimeter, while moving into position, reported seeing and engaging three Viet Cong with unknown results. Colonel Collins placed the battalion on 75 percent alert as preplanned artillery harassing fires continued.

At 2200 the Viet Cong commenced a heavy mortar attack on the small circle of U.S. troops. Within two minutes after the first explosions, countermortar fire was initiated by the heavy mortar platoons led by Sergeant First Class Kenneth D. Davis. The fire was directed to the area where it appeared the mortar attack was originating. Sergeant Davis and his platoon fired a total of 435 rounds during the battle. For some thirty minutes round after round of 120-mm., 82-mm., and 60-mm. mortar ammuntion exploded inside the base. In addition to the estimated two hundred incoming rounds, the Viet Cong employed 75-mm. recoilless rifles and RPG2 antitank weapons against the perimeter of the base. Several tracks were hit; twenty U.S. troops were wounded. Cooks, maintenance crews, and medical personnel began carrying the wounded to the airstrip; helicopters evacuated the injured as they arrived.

As soon as the mortar barrage ended, Colonel Collins directed all his units to conduct a reconnaissance by fire of the area from 200 to 600 meters beyond the perimeter. The relative stillness was shattered by the noise of .50-caliber machine guns mounted on the tracks and ground mounts. The reconnaissance by fire had no sooner ended than the enemy—two battalions in strength—launched a ground attack along the eastern sector into the positions held by A Company. It was now about 2230.

Among those firing—not now in reconnaissance, but in defense—was Staff Sergeant Richard A. Griffin of A Company. During the mortar attack Sergeant Griffin had run from his sheltered position to resupply his comrades along the perimeter with ammunition. When the ground attack began, he returned to his machine gun and placed a heavy volume of accurate fire on the enemy. He was later awarded the Bronze Star with V (valor) device.

The 3d Brigade tactical command post at Suoi Da had been requested to provide close tactical air support, artillery, medical evacuation for the wounded, and ammunition resupply. The response to these requests was immediate. Medical evacuation and resupply were provided with the dispatch of five Hueys and a light fire team. Sixty-four sorties were flown under fire into Bases I and II. With their landing lights on, the aircraft brought in sixteen tons of supplies by sling load. One hundred tactical air sorties supported the friendly forces.

In addition to the main attack from the east, the Viet Cong launched limited attacks from the northeast and southeast. Intense fire from enemy recoilless rifles and automatic weapons struck the A Company positions. Three of their armored personnel carriers were hit by enemy RPG2 rounds; one track had received a direct hit from a mortar round.

On the southwestern side of the perimeter, C Company met the enemy's secondary attack head on. Moving parallel to the highway along the western side of the road, the Viet Cong rushed across 500 meters of open ground to hit C Company's positions from the southwest. Continuous fire from the American weapons quickly gained fire superiority. The company never reported sighting more than a platoon of Viet Cong in the clearing, although many more enemy soldiers fired from the woods.

When the mortar attack had started, the artillery defensive concentrations which ringed the entire perimeter of the base were fired. As the enemy attacks commenced, adjustments in the fire were made toward and onto the attacks. Nearby artillery units at Bases I and III as well as the artillery in the Prek Klok base itself swept the area around the perimeter with over five thousand artillery rounds, while the 3d Brigade's forward air controllers directed the air strikes. An armed C–47 – "Spooky" – trained its miniguns on the Viet Cong forces to the east of the perimeter as it orbited the area.

When the first Air Force flight had arrived in the area, Route 4 was declared a fire co-ordination line between the artillery and the aircraft. To the west of the road the artillery fired and broke the enemy's assault and prohibited him from regrouping, while to the east the fighters covered the area with bombs, rockets, and 20-mm. cannon fire. The massive and devastating use of air strikes and artillery broke the back of the attack.

After an hour of fierce fighting, the brunt of the Viet Cong attack had been repelled. Sniper fire continued as the Viet Cong withdrew, and it was about 0430 before the last enemy round was fired. Early morning sweeps and aerial observation of the area disclosed 197 enemy killed. Five wounded Viet Cong were found and taken prisoner. U.S. losses were 3 killed and 38 wounded. The enemy left 12 individual weapons on the battlefield as well as a considerable amount of other equipment and gear.

It was determined that the attack had been made by two battalions of the 272d Regiment of the 9th Viet Cong Division. By now in JUNCTION CITY two of that division's regiments had attacked and been badly defeated. The remaining regiments would make their appearance in Phase II and be bloodied as well.

CHAPTER XII

Phase II—East to West

Technically speaking, JUNCTION CITY II was scheduled to begin at one minute past midnight on the morning of 18 March. However, for some elements of the U.S. 1st Infantry Division it started much earlier as they repositioned themselves and strove to complete the required facilities before the attack into eastern War Zone C began.

By 3 March, two of the three battalions of the 1st Brigade, 1st Division, which had assaulted by helicopter on D-day into the northern portion of the Phase I horseshoe, had been withdrawn from that operational area. The 1st Division engineers had completed their operations in the Phase I area by that date as well; they too were withdrawn and repositioned along the east side of War Zone C.

On 4 March the 1st Brigade, 9th U.S. Division, came under the operational control of the 1st Division. It was assigned the initial mission of opening Route 13 from Lai Khe north to Quan Loi for one or two days in order that several large convoys might pass; included in those convoys would be the men and equipment of the 1st Engineers. On 7 March the forces of the 1st Brigade, 1st Division, and of the 1st Engineers would join and the preparatory work for Phase II would commence. The mission assigned the 1st Brigade of the Big Red One was to open Route 246 west and southwest of An Loc and to secure the engineer construction party at the site where 246 crosses the Saigon River and the engineer work parties constructing the Special Forces and Civilian Irregular Defense Group camp and airfield on the west side of the river. The mission of the 1st Engineers was to improve Route 246 to the Saigon River, construct a Bailey bridge over the river, and commence construction of an airstrip just west of the bridge site. (The construction of the camp would be the responsibility of a nondivisional engineer unit.) After Phase II began, the 1st Engineers had, in addition to its usual support role, the mission of opening and maintaining Route 246 from the Bailey bridge to a fire support base which would be established at Sroc Con Trang, five kilometers northwest of the bridge.

The bridge was started on the 8th; since it was 210 feet long it was necessary to construct a concrete center pier for support. By noon on the 12th the bridge was open for traffic. By 18 March—the opening of Phase II—Route 246 had been opened and in fact improved to a distance of just over 6 kilometers west of the bridge site to the turnoff to Sroc Con Trang. By the 18th the jungle had been cleared from 1,800 feet of the runway, shaping and compacting of the subgrade continued, and 400 feet of runway had been completed. Phase II could begin.

The II Field Force mission for the second phase remained the same as for the first; all that changed was the focus of activity. During this phase, Lieutenant General Bruce Palmer, Jr., succeeded General Seaman as the commanding general of II Field Force, Vietnam.

The mission of the Big Red One for Phase II was to continue security of the bridge site and Routes 246 and 244 within the zone; to construct and secure the Special Forces and Civilian Irregular Defense Group camp and airfield; and to place two brigades astride the two enemy routes of communication in eastern War Zone C and have them conduct search and destroy operations. For resupply purposes it was also necessary to keep Route 13 open from Lai Khe to Quan Loi most of the period.

In addition to its organic 1st and 2d Brigades (Colonels Caldwell and Grimsley), the 1st Division would have available the 1st Brigade, 9th Division (Colonel Maurice W. Kendall who was succeeded by Colonel Donald A. Seibert during the period), which would remain attached until 29 March; the 173d Airborne Brigade (General Deane), attached from 20 March to 13 April; and the 11th Armored Cavalry Regiment (-) (Colonel Cobb), attached from 1 through 15 April. One of the squadrons of the 11th would be attached for the entire phase.

The mission of the 1st Brigade of the 1st Division would continue to be the security of Route 246, the bridge site, the camp and airfield, and some of the twelve fire support patrol bases the division would establish (stretching from Lai Khe north to Quan Loi, west to Sroc Con Trang, and south on Route 244 from its junction with 246). The 1st Brigade, 9th Division, except for one week, would be responsible for keeping Route 13 open from Lai Khe to Quan Loi, for escorting convoys along it, and for defending assigned fire bases in its operational area. (One such fire base at Ap Bau Bang was attacked on 20 March.) It would also conduct considerable searching and destroying—with some success— adjacent to Route 13. On 1 April the 11th Armored Cavalry Regiment (-) was to be attached to the 1st Division and would assume

GUIDING A RECOVERY VEHICLE ACROSS A RIVER

the mission of the 1st of the 9th until the end of Phase II. Escorting as many as two hundred vehicles a day through the 55-kilometer run, these units kept enemy firings upon convoys to very few (only two under the 11th Armored Cavalry with no damage). (*Map 14*)

On 17 April the 2d Brigade, 1st Division, was relieved of its Revolutionary Development operations by the 3d Brigade and joined JUNCTION CITY for the first time. Commencing on 21 March the 2d Brigade would insert two battalions into Landing Zones BRAVO and CHARLIE in Objective Area FAUST northwest of Sroc Con Trang (and only 2 kilometers south of the Cambodian border); they would conduct search and destroy operations south to Route 246. By 29 March the brigade was to secure Fire Support Patrol Base THRUST along Route 244, 1,500 meters south of its junction with Route 246. On 30 and 31 March it was to conduct airmobile assaults with at least two battalions into Landing Zone GEORGE in Objective Area SIOUX, deep in War Zone C just 5 kilometers east of Bo Tuc and 2 kilometers north of Route 246. (The battle of Ap Gu would take place in Area SIOUX on 1 April.) The 2d was also to

PHASE II—EAST TO WEST

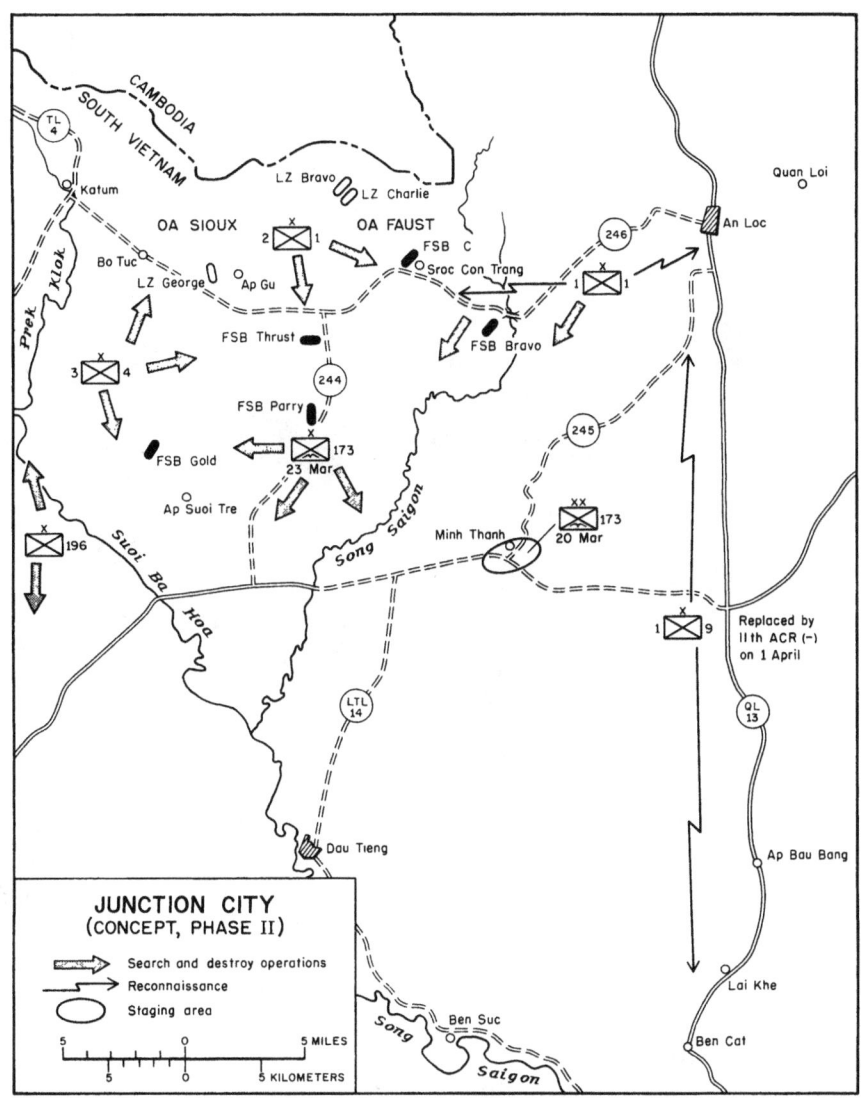

MAP 14

secure Fire Support Patrol Base C (Sroc Con Trang) and its assigned portion of Routes 246 and 244.

The 173d Airborne Brigade was not initially included among the forces to participate in Phase II; however, as soon as Phase I ended the 1st Division made representations to II Field Force for another brigade. Consequently, the 173d was attached to the Big

A UH–1D "Huey" Helicopter Prepares To Land Near Awaiting Troops

Red One on 20 March with the mission of securing the staging area at Minh Thanh and conducting airmobile assaults into eastern War Zone C beginning 23 March. On the 22d the 173d established Fire Support Patrol Base Parry near Route 244, seven kilometers south of the junction of Routes 244 and 246. From 23 March until 7 April the brigade conducted airmobile assaults and search and destroy operations southwest, west, and northwest of Parry; from 9–11 April the brigade did the same to the south and southeast of that base. On 13 April Phase II terminated for the 173d and it returned to Bien Hoa.

The mission of the 25th Infantry Division in Phase II was to continue offensive operations in War Zone C to destroy COSVN facilities and Viet Cong and North Vietnamese Army forces and installations. It was also required to secure the artillery base at the French Fort and the Special Forces and Civilian Irregular Defense Group camp and airfield at Prek Klok, keeping Route 4 open between these installations and Suoi Da. Forces to be used for these missions were the 196th Brigade and the 3d Brigade of the 4th Division.

PHASE II—EAST TO WEST

Before the end of Phase I, the 196th Brigade (General Knowles) had already assumed the mission of securing the two installations along Route 4 and keeping that road open. The brigade remained in the general area of the French Fort and Prek Klok until 28 March, during which time it conducted search and destroy operations and established blocking positions to the east of Route 4 in conjunction with a sweep being conducted by the 3d Brigade, 4th Division. Between 28 March and 7 April most of the brigade conducted "mobile brigade" operations in the northern portion of War Zone C. Moving every three or four days and conducting extensive search and destroy operations at each stop, the 196th succeeded in denying the Viet Cong freedom of access to the area. On 9 April JUNCTION CITY terminated for the 196th as it prepared to leave the II Field Force area and move north to Task Force OREGON in the I Corps zone.

In performing its mission in Phase II, the 3d Brigade, 4th Division (Colonel Garth), shifted its activities initially to the east. Its operational area was about in the center of War Zone C, bounded on the west by the 196th and on the east by the operational area of the 1st Division. On 19 March two infantry battalions and an artillery battalion (-) were airlifted into Fire Support Base GOLD, located in the southeastern portion of the operational area; one of the infantry battalions secured the base and conducted operations around it, while the other conducted operations in the area to the west of GOLD. A mechanized infantry battalion and an attached tank battalion were also assigned operational areas. (On 21 March Fire Support Base GOLD would be the site of the battle of Suoi Tre.) These forces eventually turned southeast and conducted operations back to their base camp at Dau Tieng, arriving on 8 April. On the 11th the brigade moved to an operational area in the southern portion of War Zone C north of Nui Ba Den. The 3d Brigade conducted operations in that area, as well as securing Tay Ninh city and Suoi Da, until 20 April when it returned to its base camp in Dau Tieng. On that date it was relieved of its mission by the 1st Brigade, 9th Division, and the 3d Brigade's participation in JUNCTION CITY had ended.

During the twenty-nine days of Phase II operations in which intensive searching and destruction were performed, there were only three major battles, all initiated by the enemy. There were mortar attacks upon fire bases and upon battalion positions. For example, Fire Support Patrol Base C at Sroc Con Trang, one of the largest established in JUNCTION CITY, sustained eleven mortar attacks. Enemy mining and ambush activities were conducted on Routes 246 and 244 and were mainly concentrated on either side of the junction of those two roads. Viet Cong in small three- to four-man groups could maintain continuous pressure on the roads. Although there were many contacts and some heated fire fights with enemy forces, none of these forces—except in the three battles—was significant. As the 173d Brigade found, it made contact of some type each of the twenty-two days it participated in Phase II, but the contacts were with small groups, never larger than platoon size. By the last week of this phase the enemy became increasingly more difficult to find. But this failure to dig out the enemy should not detract from the success attained by friendly forces as they continued to find and destroy installations and to discover vast amounts of supplies and equipment. All of this tended to nullify the years of labor expended by the enemy in building, digging, and tunneling and in accumulating, hauling, and hoarding supplies.

During Phase II the enemy left nearly 1,900 of his dead on the battlefield, had 19 captured, and lost over 240 weapons. And apparently in desperation for a big victory, the 9th Viet Cong Division had sacrificed its other regiments in futile attempts at the battles of Ap Bau Bang II, Suoi Tre, and Ap Gu.

CHAPTER XIII

The Battles of Ap Bau Bang II, Suoi Tre, and Ap Gu

Ap Bau Bang II

At 1150 on 19 March 1967, A Troop, 3d Squadron, 5th Cavalry Regiment, commanded by Captain Raoul H. Alcala, deployed within the perimeter of Fire Support Base 20. A unit of the 1st Brigade, 9th Infantry, attached to the 1st Infantry Division, the 129-man company had six tanks, twenty M-113 armored personnel carriers, and three 4.2-inch mortar carriers. The unit formed into a circular (wagon train) perimeter defense with the mission of securing the base for B Battery (105-mm.) of the 7th Battalion, 9th Artillery, commanded by Captain Duane W. Marion.

Fire Support Base 20 was located in relatively flat country 1,500 meters north of Ap Bau Bang immediately west of QL 13. To the south of the position was a rubber plantation, while wooded areas were prominent to the north and west. An abandoned railroad track ran parallel to and thirty meters east of the highway. (*Map 15*)

Intelligence sources had indicated that the Ap Bau Bang area was infested with local force guerrillas; they had also pointed out a well-used trail to the north which ran east and west. Captain Alcala sent his 2d Platoon commanded by First Lieutenant Harlan E. Short to establish an ambush along the trail at a point 1,500 meters north of the fire support base and approximately 350 meters west of Route 13. The ambush was to be in position by 1800. The perimeter was manned on the west by the 1st Platoon, commanded by First Lieutenant Roger A. Festa; occupying the eastern portion was the 3d Platoon under Second Lieutenant Hiram M. Wolfe, IV.

At 2250 that night a Viet Cong probe signaled the start of the second battle of Ap Bau Bang. The probe was spearheaded by a herd of fifteen belled cattle being driven across Route 13 at a point 150 meters northeast of the perimeter. Ten minutes later the Viet Cong started raking the northeast section of the perimeter with a wheel-mounted .50-caliber machine gun located on the railroad track embankment. Specialist Four Eugene W. Stevens, command-

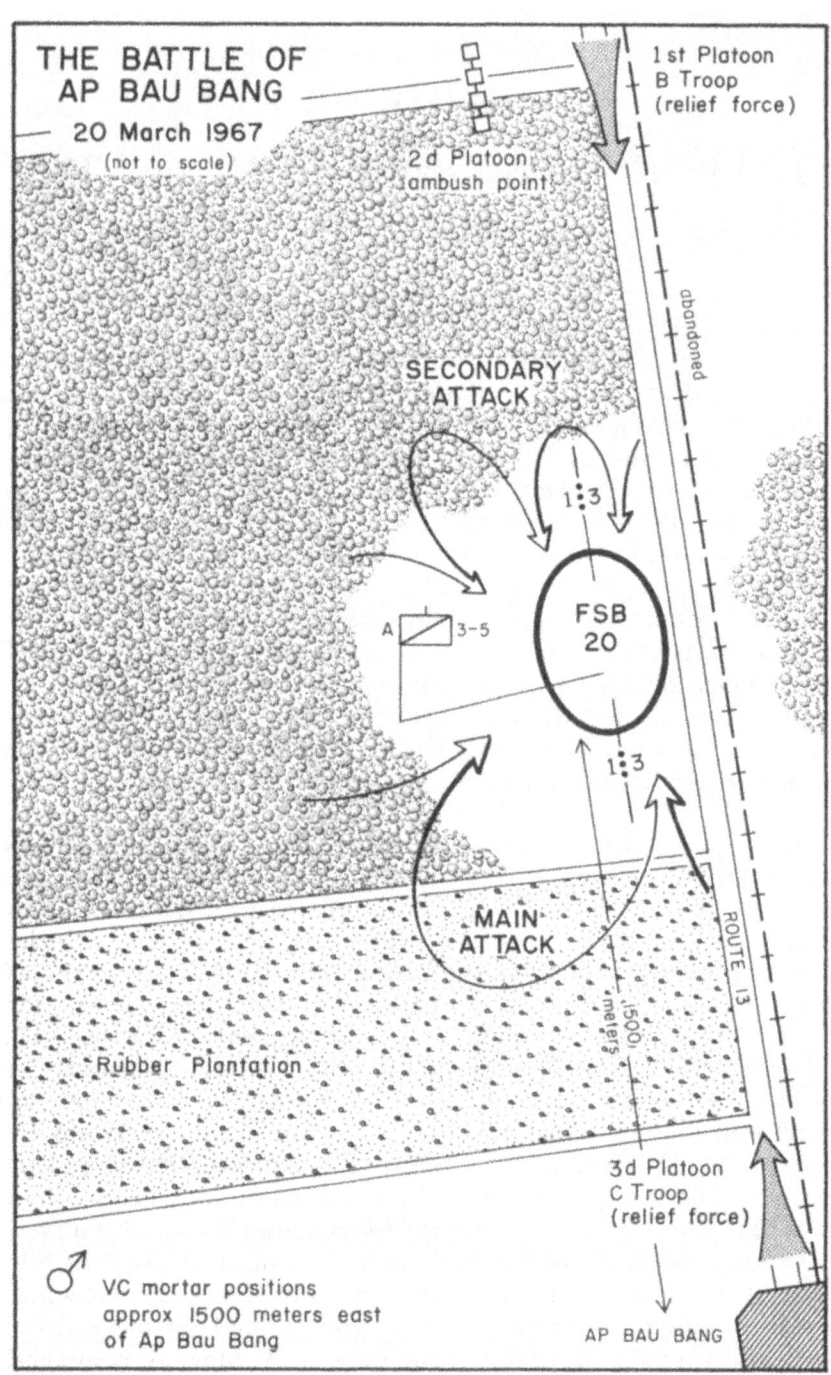

MAP 15

ing one of the tanks, trained his searchlight on the Viet Cong position and returned the fire with all his weapons. The fire fight was joined by the weapons of three of the APC's and continued for about three minutes. The enemy gun sprayed the perimeter with only five separate bursts of fire before it was silenced by the response of A troop.

During the lull that followed, the units, including the 2d Platoon still manning the ambush site, assumed a state of increased readiness. Reconaissance by fire was conducted by Lieutenant Wolfe's tank along the wood line to the east beyond the railroad. At 2310 Captain Alcala reported: "Firing has ceased now, we are using infra-red to scan the area for movement. . . ."

At 0030, 20 March 1967, the Viet Cong attack resumed as Fire Support Base 20 was hit with mortar rounds, rifle grenades, rockets, and recoilless rifle fire. The beginning of the main phase of the battle had been signaled. Lieutenant Festa's track was hit, wounding his sergeant. It was apparent that the Viet Cong were well zeroed in. The fire was now coming from the west. Captain Alcala requested artillery support from the battalion he was securing and from Lai Khe.

Brigadier General James F. Hollingsworth, assistant division commander of the 1st Infantry Division, later described this phase of the battle:

> Their mortar positions were located from 1500 to 2000 meters west of Ap Bau Bang in and around an old village that had been destroyed. The mortar positions were located by radar from the Lai Khe artillery oase. . . . I understood the counter mortar radar played an important role in picking them up. However, the most accurate way of picking up the mortars during this battle was by two airborne artillery observers who could see the flashes from the mortars. I think that a combination of both brought about their location.

As the instensity of the fire increased, another M-113 was hit. Then another APC received direct hits in the front and left side from recoilless rifle rounds; three of the crew were wounded and the vehicle was set afire. Two of the 3d Platoon tanks were hit; however, both remained in the battle.

Throughout the mortar and antitank bombardment, Captain Alcala maintained radio contact with his squadron commander, Lieutenant Colonel Sidney S. Haszard, located to the south.

Within twenty minutes of the beginning of the mortar attack, the Viet Cong ground assault began with the main attack coming from the south and southwest and with a secondary attack from the north. The massed troops of the 273d Viet Cong Regiment emerged from the rubber trees and moved steadily forward under a base of fire. The enemy soldiers were wearing black pajamas or dark colored fatigues and sandals, and carrying individual weapons. The attack was co-ordinated with the mortar fire, and not until the enemy came out in the open was its magnitude apparent.

Captain Alcala advised his headquarters at 0050 that he could handle the attack, but asked that a ready reaction force be set up in case it was needed. Colonel Haszard acknowledged the message and alerted the 1st Platoon of B Troop to the north of Ap Bau Bang and the 3d Platoon of C Troop to the south to move to Fire Support Base 20. He gave Captain Alcala permission to alert his 2d Platoon at the ambush site to prepare for movement back into the perimeter. Colonel Haszard noted the growing size of the enemy offensive and decided to move with his command element to A Troop's position.

In the 3d Platoon sector on the eastern side of the perimeter, Lieutenant Wolfe detected Viet Cong movement and requested night illumination from a 4.2-inch mortar. As the light from the flare swung across the area, it was possible to see Viet Cong troops crossing the highway from east to west. The platoon commenced firing and the enemy movement stopped. Staff Sergeant George Hua reported, "I got two hits on top of my turret from 60mm mortar rounds, 2 rounds struck the gun shield below the gun tube. . . . Another round hit the main gun's blast deflector, so we opened fire with everything we could lay our hands on."

At 0100 Captain Alcala was advised that a flareship—Spooky 742—armed with miniguns, and a light fire team of helicopter gunships were on the way.

The enemy troops on the southwest portion of the perimeter were starting to swarm over some of the APC's. A voice from Track 10 came to Staff Sergeant Dorren in Track 17: "They are swarming all over my track. Dust me with canister." Sergeant Dorren hesitated, concerned about the effects of canister on the crew. Once again came the plea, "My people are down, shoot!" Several rounds of canister wiped out the enemy in the area of the overrun track. Staff Sergeant Ramos-Rasario also called for a dusting by canister. Sergeant Dorren fired several rounds in front of Track 11, eliminating the Viet Cong. Another call for help came from Track 10. Sergeant Dorren fired again and then watched the track burst into a ball of fire as enemy mortar rounds scored direct hits. The wounded crew escaped, but Private First Class Steve Lopez died later of his wounds.

Two more armored personnel carriers were hit, one of them Lieutenant Wolfe's track. Because the Viet Cong were in so close to his line of APC's, Wolfe had to pull back about twenty-five or thirty meters and realign the platoon, completing the move by 0115. Lieutenant Wolfe's track was hit a second time by an RPG2 rocket. The entire crew was wounded and evacuated to the medical clearing tent in the center of the perimeter.

The troop's 2d Platoon came charging down Route 13 from its ambush site, the men firing intermittently as they came. The troopers, after arriving at the fire support base, manned the gaps in the hard-pressed southern half of the perimeter. As they took their positions, they were hit with recoilless rifle fire and grenades.

The elements of B and C Troops alerted earlier received the order to move and immediately raced to join the battle. The 3d Platoon of C Troop, attacking up Route 13 from its troop's position five kilometers to the south, ran through a barrage of enemy fire before reaching the perimeter at 0127. At the direction of Captain Alcala, the platoon swept 1,500 meters south of the defenders along the rubber-grove tree line. Firing continually during their sweep, the cavalrymen swung west, then north, then doubled back and entered the perimeter from the southeast. The vehicles pulled into positions between A Troop's vehicles on the eastern portion of the perimeter defense.

At this same time the 1st Platoon of B Troop was tearing down Route 13 from its position eight kilometers north. After blasting through a hastily built ambush just north of the perimeter, the troopers moved around to the south, firing as they went. Moving into the perimeter, the platoon took up positions between A Troop's vehicles on the western half of the defensive ring.

The perimeter now contained the artillery battery, all of A Troop, and the two relief platoons—a large quantity of armor for the size of the perimeter. Captain Alcala expanded the perimeter by forty meters with a counterattack at 0220.

Two of the tracks hit previously continued to burn throughout the engagement. Lieutenant Festa moved forward with two APC's to evacuate the wounded lying nearby. Several Viet Cong attempting to remove the .50-caliber machine gun from one of the burning tracks were killed, as were others attacking the foxholes containing the wounded. Lieutenant Festa and Specialist Four Abelardo Penedo, while under intense fire, dismounted and loaded the wounded into Festa's personnel carrier.

Meanwhile Colonel Haszard, in an APC followed by another M–113 bearing his command group, moved up Route 13 to the perimeter. Just short of the perimeter, Haszard's track was hit and disabled. Captain Alcala sent a tank out of the perimeter to assist the disabled track. Colonel Haszard dismounted in heavy small arms fire and, warding off the Viet Cong, attached the towline. The command track, with its valuable communications equipment, was pulled into the perimeter.

At 0300 another attack was developing to the south of the perimeter. It appeared to Captain Alcala that this attack was an attempt by the Viet Cong to recover bodies. Behind a line of skirmishers, unarmed troops advanced carrying ropes and wires with hooks attached to recover the bodies left on the battlefield. The attacking force was stopped within fifteen meters of the perimeter.

During this attack, and for the next four hours, miniguns and air strikes pounded the Viet Cong from above. An Air Force flareship kept the battle area continually lighted. Initially the artillery covered the northwest, west, and southwest sides of the perimeter while aircraft attacked on a north-south axis east of Route 13. Later a switch was made and the aircraft attack runs were made from east to west on the south and southwest sides of the perimeter.

During the battle, resupply and "Dust-off" (medical evacuation) missions continued under the direction of Lieutenant Colonel Paul F. Gorman, G–3 of the 1st Infantry Division. Because of the nature of the battle and the preponderance of automatic weapons on armored vehicles, two and in some cases three basic loads of .50-caliber and 7.62-mm. ammunition were expended during the fight. At 0330 the enemy fire slackened; resupply of the units and evacuation of the wounded was completed during the next hour and fifteen minutes while the artillery and air strikes continued. Twenty-six of the sixty-three men wounded were evacuated; many of the slightly wounded chose to stay in their positions and man their weapons.

By 0450 it was noted under the illumination of flares and tank searchlights that the enemy was massing for an attack on the south and southeast sides of the perimeter. The Viet Cong started their attack at 0500; the artillery shifted its fire to the west, and aircraft dropped cluster bomb units followed by napalm and 500-pound bombs on the attackers. The final assault of the Viet Cong was blunted and the noises of battle subsided. At 0700 the final air strike and artillery rounds were placed on the withdrawing enemy.

Colonel Haszard delivered the following message to the men who had taken part in the battle:

> I am extremely proud of every man in this unit for [his] actions last night. However, there are still many VC in the area. Therefore, you must take all precautions. I want you to have reaction forces ready for all elements in the way that you did today. . . . Sweep operations tomorrow must be done thoroughly. Insure that perimeters tonight are the best possible.

AP BAU BANG II, SUOI TRE, AND AP GU   135

The battle of Ap Bau Bang II[1] resulted in 227 (known) enemy dead, 3 prisoners taken, and the capture of much enemy equipment and weapons. Blood trails stood as mute evidence of the many bodies hauled away by the Viet Cong. Although more enemy than usual are killed by small arms when attacks are made on cavalry and armored units, the majority of enemy deaths in this battle, as in others, resulted from artillery and air strikes. In this instance, 29 air strikes delivered 29 tons of ordnance, and the artillery fired nearly 3,000 rounds. U.S. battle losses were 3 men killed and 63 wounded. Enemy prisoners identified the attackers as the 2d and 3d Battalions of the 273d Regiment of the 9th Viet Cong Division. Intelligence experts believed the whole regiment participated.

As a result of the battle, General Hay wrote a letter to the 9th Division commander. Printed in Vietnamese in leaflet form, it was dropped into the enemy area. Translated, the text of the letter read:

This is to advise you that during the battle of Ap Bau Bang on 20 March the Regimental Commander of Q763 (273d Regiment) and his Battalion Commanders disgraced themselves by performing in an unsoldierly manner.

During this battle with elements of this Division and attached units your officers failed to accomplish their mission and left the battlefield covered with dead and wounded from their units.

We have buried your dead and taken care of your wounded from this battle.

The letter bore the signature of General J. H. Hay.

Suoi Tre

The target for the helicopters was an egg-shaped clearing close to Suoi Tre, near the center of War Zone C and ninety kilometers northwest of Saigon. It was just three kilometers away from the area in which, during Operation ATTLEBORO four months earlier, the 1st Battalion, 28th Infantry, of the U.S. 1st Division had defeated elements of the 272d Viet Cong and 101st North Vietnamese Regiments at the battle of Ap Cha Do. Events would reveal that the 272d had returned.

On 19 March, in an area surrounded by a tree line of sparse woodland which had been blighted by defoliants, U.S. helicopters

---

[1] Ap Bau Bang was also the site of the first major Vietnam action in which the 1st Infantry Division participated on 12 November 1965. In Ap Bau Bang I the 272d and 273d Regiments of the 9th Viet Cong Division attacked the 2d Battalion, 2d Infantry (-), defensive perimeter and were repelled with the assistance of air strikes and direct fire artillery at the cost to the Viet Cong of 198 killed.

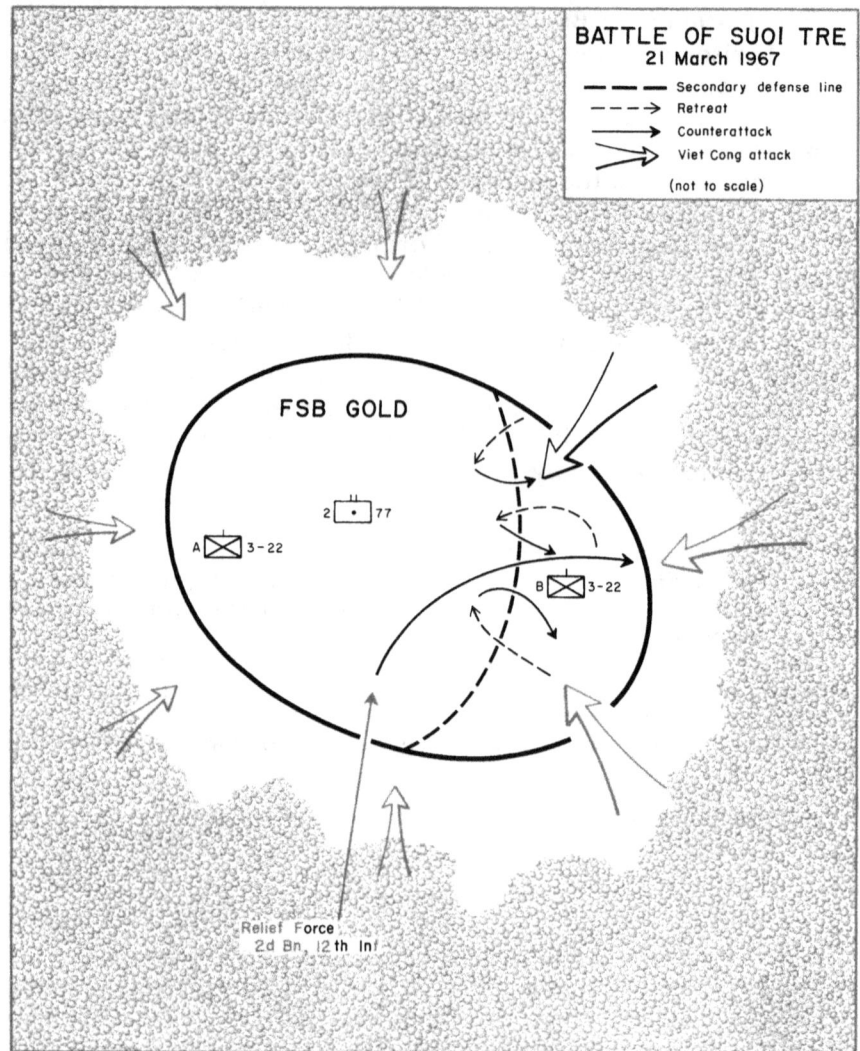

MAP 16

airlanded the 3d Battalion of the 22d Infantry and the 2d Battalion, 77th Artillery (–), led by Lieutenant Colonels John A. Bender and John W. Vessey, Jr., respectively, under the control of the 3d Brigade, 4th Infantry Division (Colonel Garth). Their mission was to establish a fire support base (GOLD) in support of Phase II of JUNCTION CITY. Heavy action was not expected. However, from the outset it was apparent that things would be different at Suoi Tre. (*Map 16*)

As the three lifts of choppers touched down, five heavy command-detonated charges were set off by the Viet Cong in the tiny clearing. Three helicopters were destroyed and 6 more damaged with a toll of 15 killed and 28 wounded.[2] A Viet Cong claymore-type mine was also detonated against C Company of the 3d Battalion, wounding 5 infantrymen.

Company B of the 3d Battalion, 22d Infantry, was assigned the east portion of the defensive perimeter, Company A the western half. Later that day the 2d Battalion, 12th Infantry, landed at Fire Support Base GOLD and moved to the northwest. Its last lift drew enemy fire, and another seven choppers were damaged.

Work progressed rapidly on 20 March to improve the fire support base perimeter defenses, and fortunate it was for the occupants of the base. The battle of Suoi Tre was to begin the next day.

At 0430 a night patrol from Company B operating outside the battalion perimeter reported movement around its ambush site. Minutes—then hours—passed and no further movement was detected. At 0630 the patrol prepared to return to camp. One minute later the area exploded as the base came under heavy attack from enemy 60-mm. and 82-mm. mortars. At the same time the patrol was attacked by a massive Viet Cong force. Within five minutes the patrol had been overrun, and all of its men were killed or wounded.

The first enemy mortar round had impacted on the doorstep of a company command post; seconds later another exploded outside battalion headquarters. In all, an estimated 650 mortar rounds fell while the Viet Cong advanced toward the perimeter. As they moved closer, enemy machine guns and recoilless rifles joined

---

[2] On the following day, 20 March, a similar misfortune might well have occurred in the 1st Division's area. There the 1st Battalion, 26th Infantry, had moved by foot to seize Sroc Con Trang which was to become Fire Support Patrol Base C for Phase II of JUNCTION CITY. It was unusual for the forces of the Big Red One not to make an airmobile assault into such an area. However, on 30 June 1966 the 1st Division had captured a Viet Cong plan to attack and annihilate a U.S. battalion on a landing zone at Sroc Con Trang. After the 1st of the 26th had secured the area, the 36th South Vietnamese Ranger Battalion, among other units, occupied and helped secure it. On 21 March the 36th Rangers discovered batteries and a wire in the wood line near the fire support base; following the wire, they found four holes filled with explosives. There was a center hole, and radiating from it was wire leading to three other holes at a distance of about twenty-five meters. In each hole were the necessary detonating caps. In the center one were also the following rounds: eight 75-mm., seven 81-mm., fourteen 60-mm., and 105 pounds of TNT. The other holes had similar but smaller loads: only 35 pounds of TNT each and various numbers and types of U.S. ordnance. It was all set to be command detonated. From then on the Big Red One, when it placed artillery and air strike preparatory fires around and into any landing zone into which it was bringing troops, always used a number of instantaneous fuzed bombs to strike the planned landing site of its chopper lifts in order to cut any wires and yet not chew up the terrain so much that it would be difficult to land and traverse.

the attack. The Viet Cong made final preparations to assault the position.

Within minutes the entire perimeter came under heavy attack by waves of Viet Cong emerging from the jungle and firing recoilless rifles, RPG2 rockets, automatic weapons, and small arms. The heaviest attacks were concentrated on the northeastern and southeastern portions of the defensive perimeter. As the attack increased in intensity, the three artillery batteries initiated countermortar fire in an effort to neutralize the heavy mortar concentrations which continued to rake the position. During the first assault Company B reported that its 1st Platoon positions on the southeastern perimeter had been penetrated and that the reaction force from the 2d Battalion, 77th Artillery, was needed to reinforce that sector. Artillerymen responded to the call, rushing to the perimeter to help repulse the continuing attacks.

At 0700 the first forward air controller arrived overhead in a light observation aircraft and immediately began directing Air Force strikes against the attackers. At the same time, supporting fire from two batteries of 105-mm. howitzers located at nearby fire support bases was brought within one hundred meters of the battalion's perimeter. At 0711, Company B reported that its 1st Platoon had been overrun and surrounded by a human-wave attack. Air strikes were called in all along the wood line to the east to relieve the pressure on the company's perimeter. The forward air controller directing these strikes was shot down by heavy automatic weapons fire. At 0750 the Company B commander requested that the artillery fire its "beehive" rounds (canisters filled with hundreds of metal darts) into the southeastern and southern sections of his perimeter. At 0756 Company B reported that complete enemy penetration had been made in the 1st Platoon sector and that they were desperate for ammunition resupply. Ammunition and a 20-man reaction force from Company A were sent to assist B Company. At 0813 the northeastern section of the perimeter was overrun by another human-wave attack. Two minutes later, elements of Company A which had established an ambush just outside the perimeter the previous night charged into the camp's perimeter and assumed defensive positions. Somehow all of the men had managed to elude the surrounding Viet Cong.

The commander of Company A reported the Viet Cong had penetrated the northern sector of the perimeter. Ten minutes later a quad-.50 machine gun located in that sector of the base was hit by RPG2 rocket rounds and overrun. As the attacking Viet Cong swarmed over the weapon and attempted to turn it on the friendly positions, the gun was blown apart by a well-placed round from a 105-mm. howitzer crew who had witnessed the whole action from their position some seventy-five meters away. By 0840 the northeastern, eastern, and southeastern portions of the perimeter had withdrawn to a secondary defensive line around the guns of the artillery batteries. The northern, western, and southern sectors were managing to hold despite intense pressure from large numbers of Viet Cong who had advanced as close as fifteen meters from the defensive positions. Attackers had infiltrated to within hand grenade range of the battalion command post and only five meters from the battalion aid station.

The howitzers of the artillery battalion, with their tubes leveled, began firing beehive rounds into the Viet Cong. At point-blank range, round after round of direct fire was delivered, each round spewing 8,000 finned steel missiles into the enemy.

Air strikes were brought within as little as fifty meters of U.S. forces, and supporting artillery batteries threw up a continuous wall of shrapnel around the battalion perimeter. When the artillery inside the perimeter had exhausted its supply of beehive rounds, it began to fire high explosive rounds at point-blank range. By 0900 the northern, western, and southern sectors of the perimeter were holding but still under Viet Cong pressure. The positions on the east had withdrawn even closer, but the line was still intact.

The 3d Brigade headquarters had earlier alerted its other units which were conducting operations to the west. They were the 2d Battalion, 12th Infantry; the mechanized 2d Battalion, 22d Infantry; and the 2d Battalion, 34th Armor (–). When word of the attack reached these forces, they reacted immediately. The 2d of the 12th moved from the northwest traveling cross-country and avoiding traveled roads and trails. The mechanized infantry and armor battalions moved from the southwest until they reached the Suoi (stream) Samat. An intensive search revealed only one suitable fording site.

At 0900 the relief column from the 2d of the 12th broke through and linked up with the battered Company B. With the added forces and firepower, the units were able to counterattack to the east and re-establish the original perimeter. But the Viet Cong were still attacking. As they advanced, many of the soldiers could be seen wearing bandages from earlier wounds. Some, so badly wounded that they could not walk, were carried piggyback into the assaults by their comrades.

Twelve minutes after the first relief unit arrived, the mechanized infantry and armor column broke through the jungle from the southwest. With their 90-mm. guns firing canister rounds and all machine guns blazing, they moved into the advancing Viet

Cong, cutting them down. Shortly thereafter, the enemy began to withdraw. By 0930 the original perimeter had been re-established and by 1000 resupply choppers were arriving and began evacuating the wounded. By 1045 the battle of Suoi Tre was over. Elements of the mechanized and armor battalions pursued the fleeing enemy, and artillery and air strikes continued to pound routes of withdrawal. Sporadic contact continued until noon.

The attacking unit had been decimated; 647 bodies were recovered, 7 prisoners were taken, and 65 crew-served and 94 individual weapons were captured. (Of the weapons captured, 50 were RPG2's, a small bazooka-type antitank weapon.) U.S. losses were 31 killed and 109 wounded.

Documents found in the area showed that intensive planning had been made by the Viet Cong before the attack. The attacking force was identified as the 272d Regiment of the 9th Viet Cong Division reinforced by elements of U-80 Artillery. The 272d was considered one of the best organized and equipped enemy units and was one of the few Viet Cong units that dared to make daylight attacks. But at Suoi Tre its troops had been scattered in a disorganized route to the northeast with artillery and air strikes pounding at their heels.

Ap Gu

On 26 March the 1st Battalion, 26th Infantry (the Blue Spaders), commanded by Lieutenant Colonel Alexander M. Haig, was alerted to prepare for an assault deeper into War Zone C and near the Cambodian border. At that time the battalion was attached to the 2d Brigade of the 1st Division and was located at Fire Support Patrol Base C at Sroc Con Trang. There it was engaged in perimeter defense, road security, and occasional search and destroy operations. Now Colonel Haig turned his S-3 loose on the planning for the assault. It was to be made in late morning on the 30th into Landing Zone GEORGE, some fourteen kilometers to the west in Operational Area SIOUX. The Blue Spaders would secure the zone for a follow-up landing by the 1st Battalion, 2d Infantry, and then conduct operations in their assigned sector. Intelligence indicated that they could expect to make contact with the enemy in that area. (*Map 17*)

On the day scheduled for the assault, poor weather delayed the preparatory air strikes around and on the landing zone, resulting in a two-hour delay in H-hour. (The assault of the 1st of the 2d was postponed a day.) It was not until early afternoon that the initial elements of the battalion touched down at GEORGE. (The landing

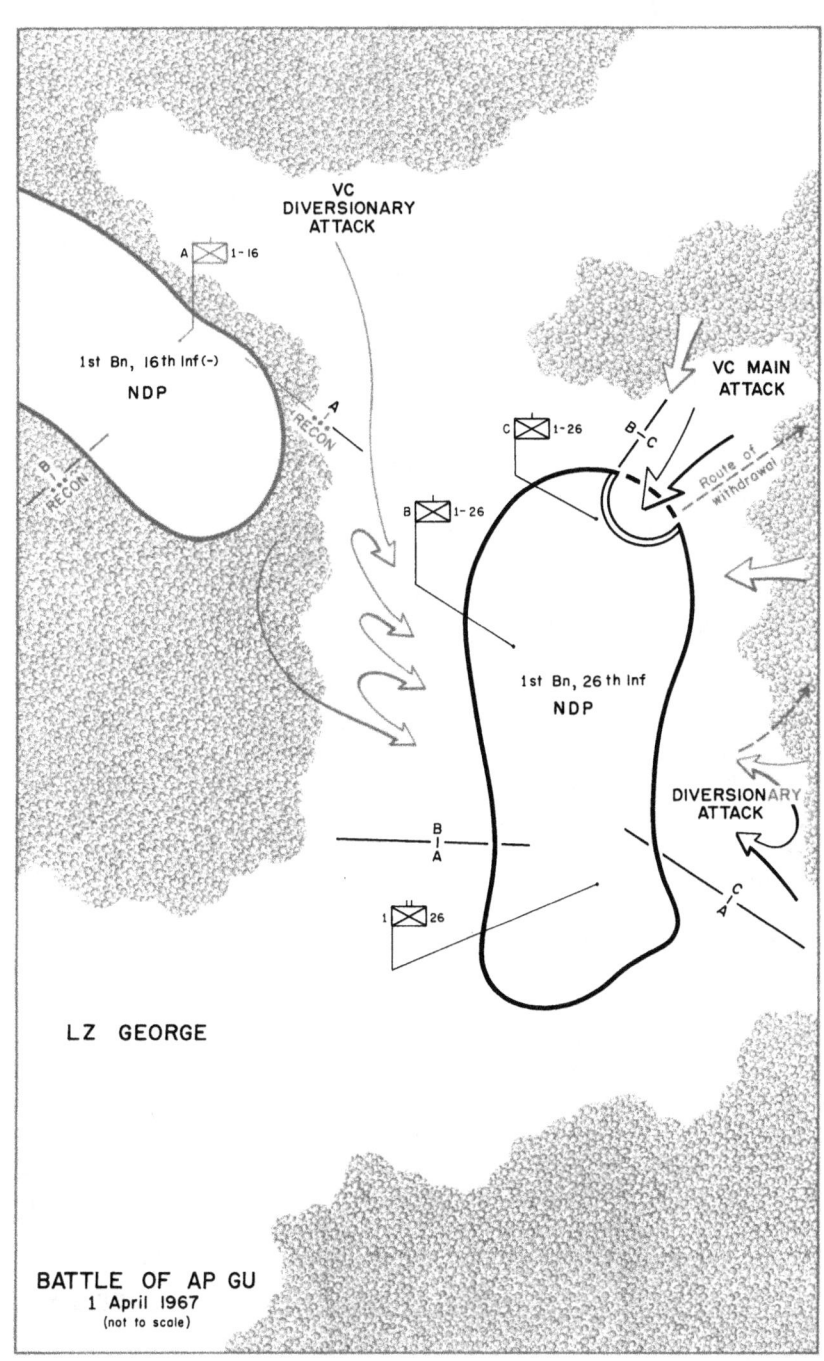

BATTLE OF AP GU
1 April 1967
(not to scale)

MAP 17

zone terrain consisted of open fields covered with tall, meadow-like grass. The area was surrounded by medium to heavy jungle.) The remainder of the battalion closed within an hour. Upon landing the battalion immediately dispatched cloverleaf patrols to seek the enemy. The patrols uncovered fortified positions in and around the landing zone; however, they made no contact. That evening the unit organized its night defensive position in the vicinity of the zone. Fighting positions were dug as always with full overhead cover and interlocking fires all around. Listening posts were established and ambush patrols sent out. No significant contacts occurred that night.

The next morning, 31 March, the 1st Battalion, 2d Infantry (Lieutenant Colonel William C. Simpson commanding), was airlanded in GEORGE without incident. Upon landing, the 1st of the 2d moved to a position two kilometers southwest of the landing zone. The 1st Battalion, 26th Infantry, began search and destroy operations in the surrounding area. Company A went south and C Company east. B Company remained in reserve, manning and patrolling the battalion perimeter at the landing zone.

The battalion's reconnaissance platoon was searching the woods northwest of the perimeter. There it became obvious that the Americans were expected: from the trees hung small signs written in English warning that Americans going beyond the signs would not return.

At 1300 the platoon moved farther to the north into a wooded area and was approximately five kilometers south of the Cambodian border when first contact was made. The platoon's point man was hit by enemy fire. First Lieutenant Richard A. Hill, an infantry officer experienced in Vietnam combat, went forward to check the situation and was hit and mortally wounded. Only Hill's radio operator was left in contact with the battalion S-3. Before being hit, Hill had advised the battalion that the platoon was heavily engaged with automatic weapons, small arms, and grenades. Colonel Haig had called for artillery support and, when advised that the platoon leader had been hit, immediately took action to co-ordinate the artillery fire and air strikes in support of the platoon.

At the same time, B Company was just closing on the perimeter after a sweep of the battalion's defensive area. When advised of the reconnaissance platoon's desperate position and that its leader had been hit, the commander on his own initiative swung his company to the north and proceeded to the assistance of the embattled platoon.

Colonel Haig boarded his helicopter, and it was not until he was airborne that he learned of B Company's move north. As Haig pointed out later, while this move to extract the platoon was necessary, the lack of accurate control of artillery fires and air support complicated the problem. As a result, B Company had entered the engagement without sufficient preparation and found itself heavily engaged along with the reconnaissance platoon.

The B Company commander confirmed that he was confronting at least a battalion-size enemy force. His initially optimistic reports became progressively more pessimistic; the company was pinned down by heavy machine gun fire, rockets, mortars, and recoilless rifles, and was running low on ammunition. Colonel Haig realized that he must reinforce and extract the units.

Company A was alerted for action and moved forward to pass through and relieve B Company.

Colonel Haig landed near the point of contact and had his battalion operations officer go airborne to control fire direction. Haig found Lieutenant Hill dead and the B Company commander wounded and in mild shock. Electing to stay with his units, Colonel Haig was joined by the A Company commander who had moved his unit through B Company and gained fire superiority over the enemy force.

The intensity and accuracy of artillery and air strikes increased, permitting all units, except initially two platoons of A Company still in contact, to be extracted. As the units moved back, the Viet Cong left their bunkers and moved forward to maintain contact; they were finally forced to terminate the engagement because of exposure to the incoming bombardment. Contact was broken at 1705. The engagement resulted in seven Americans killed and thirty-eight wounded. Enemy casualties were unknown at that time.

Meanwhile the division commander, General Hay, had ordered reinforcements into the area. At 1555 the first element of the 1st Battalion, 16th Infantry, minus C Company, touched down at Landing Zone GEORGE under heavy sniper fire and occupied positions to the west and northwest of the 1st of the 26th. The battalion, under Colonel Lazzell, established its night defensive positions. The two battalions co-ordinated defensive plans, improved their fighting positions, established listening posts, and sent out ambush patrols.

During the night, friendly harassment and interdiction artillery and mortar fires were placed in the area around the perimeter. From midnight until 0400 on 1 April, listening posts to the north, east, and south reported some movement to their front; however, there was no significant contact. Mortar fire was directed into areas of suspected enemy activity.

At 0455 a single enemy mortar round exploded to the front of the perimeter of the 1st Battalion, 26th Infantry. Colonel Haig heard it and correctly interpreted it to be a registration round for a Viet Cong mortar attack. He immediately ordered all of his companies to a full alert posture and directed them to take cover and be prepared for an attack. He also recommended that the 1st of the 16th follow suit. Colonel Lazzell's "Rangers" concurred and manned their fighting positions.

Colonel Haig immediately requested artillery fire for east of his position.

Five minutes after the enemy registration round had detonated, the first of several hundred rounds of 60-mm., 82-mm., and 120-mm. mortar rounds were fired into the northern portions of the battalions' areas. The rounds came from a position estimated to be a thousand meters northeast of the defensive perimeter. The mortars were so close that the U.S. troops could hear the rounds being fired. So many mortars were firing at once that the noise they made "sounded like loud, heavy machine guns." Because of the early warning, the rapid response to the first enemy round fired, and the defensive strength of the fighting positions, only twelve men were wounded.

At the same time the mortar attack opened on the units in Landing Zone GEORGE, a co-ordinated attack started on Fire Support Patrol Base C, where much of the supporting artillery for the 1st of the 26th and the 1st of the 16th was dug in. With the incoming mortar and 75-mm. pack howitzer rounds exploding around them, the artillerymen were not so efficient as usual in getting off the requested fires. However, they did not cease firing. In addition, the artillery that had moved into Fire Support Patrol Base THRUST on 29 March was not under incoming mortar attack so that it could —and did—provide the usual support to Colonels Haig and Lazzell. Why the enemy did not bring this base under attack has never come to light, but it was a mistake on his part.

When asked later about his immediate response to the registering mortar round, Colonel Haig replied that he had sensed the ultimate ground attack, but not its extent or the size of the force involved. He felt, as he was sure the Viet Cong commander felt, that they had unfinished business as a result of the action the day before. "There were indicators available to both sides that follow-up action might be appropriate, and in the VC's case, especially in view of the fact that he had four or five battalions to employ

. . . I [also] was set to exploit what I thought had been a fairly successful action the day before." There was little question that another engagement was imminent; if not instigated by the Viet Cong, then Colonel Haig would have taken the initiative.

The heavy mortar attack on the two battalions ended at 0515. (It lasted an hour longer at Fire Support Patrol Base C.) During this time flareships, a light helicopter fire team, and forward air controllers were requested from and furnished by the 2d Brigade tactical headquarters. Seven minutes later the Viet Cong launched their initial ground attack against the northeast edge of the perimeter.

The attack hit primarily B and C Companies of the 1st Battalion, 26th Infantry, and A Company and the reconnaissance platoon of the 1st Battalion, 16th Infantry. As the soldiers manning the friendly listening posts withdrew to the perimeter, the enemy had followed them in.

Private First Class William Trickett, a fire team leader in C Company, described the attack:

When the listening post came back in, they hit their [own] trip flares. . . . An [enemy] automatic weapon opened up on them and I fired my M-79 – I believe I hit and silenced her. [The VC] came on in and wound up in the 1st Platoon area. It was a mix up after dark. The next thing we know they're sprawling all over the field. Some way or another they came through our trip flares and were already in the field digging positions. . . . We lost one of our machine guns that was hit by a mortar. The other one kept firing, but considering the people we had on the listening post and everything, our positions were just under strength – we just got hit. They realized our weakness and came through us.

It was apparent that the co-ordination of mortar fire with the unobserved movement of the enemy through the woods and tall grass immediately ahead of C Company had permitted surprise in their attack resulting in the capture of three bunkers and a penetration roughly forty meters deep and a hundred meters wide in the C Company sector. Decisive hand-to-hand fighting was taking place in the penetration.

(Colonel Haig later indicated that he had known from the day he selected the night defensive position that the natural wood line leading into the northeast portion of the perimeter was the most vulnerable portion of his perimeter. He realized that he was up against a very intelligent enemy when the commander picked this spot for his attack.)

As described by Captain George A. Jones, S-3 of the battalion, the Viet Cong ". . . walked right through our mortar fire and artillery fire – they just kept coming so we knew we had a very large force out there. Charlie Company was fighting hand to hand in the bunkers as was our Bravo Company. . . . We organized about seventy-five meters back . . . consolidated the line, and held."

The commander of Company C, Captain Brian H. Cundiff, without regard to the intense enemy fire, moved among his men and mustered an effective defense which held the shoulders of the penetration. During this time he also killed six of the attacking enemy in hand-to-hand combat. Although wounded three times, he refused medical aid and continued to fight and rally his force.

At 0630 the reserve of the 1st Battalion, 26th Infantry, the reconnaissance platoon, was moved into a blocking position behind C Company and, along with B Company, fought to re-establish the perimeter. Meanwhile the enemy was launching diversionary attacks from the east and west.

The Air Force air strikes were now arriving over the target area at the rate of one flight each fifteen minutes, thus providing continuous air cover. Initially there was some difficulty in getting the flights armed with cluster bomb units.[3]

It appeared that slowly the main Viet Cong attack was beginning to falter under the heavy volume of fire placed upon it. Light and heavy helicopter fire teams were firing rockets and miniguns on the wood line to the northeast; artillery was massing fires along the east flank and in depth to the east. As the flights started arriving with cluster bomb units on board, the jets began striking within thirty meters of the American positions, littering the entire area on both sides of the perimeter with enemy dead.[4] As the ordnance began taking its toll, the Viet Cong started to run, many of them throwing down their weapons.

In the meantime, Captain Cundiff led elements of C Company, reinforced by the 1st Platoon of B Company, in a massive counterattack which was pushing the remaining Viet Cong back into the deadly artillery barrages and air strikes. By 0800 the perimeter was restored.

As the Viet Cong broke contact and began withdrawing, the 1st of the 2d and 1st of the 16th passed through the 1st of the 26th to pursue the enemy to the east and northeast. However, no significant contact was made. Artillery and air strikes (including two

---

[3] Cluster bomb units were badly needed since they were the most effective ordnance for the situation which existed: enemy troops in the open, echeloned in depth, and in contact with our own troops. Since the pilot can release the small bomb units from their cannister at low level, he can drop them within thirty meters of our own troops, and, when they explode on contact, our troops are unharmed, since the lethal radius of the ordnance is slightly less than that distance.

[4] After the battle there was one string of twenty-nine enemy dead in a line 150 meters long; a cluster bomb unit run had literally curled them up.

INFANTRYMEN OF THE 1ST INFANTRY DIVISION *dash from helicopters to move against enemy forces of the 9th Viet Cong Division.*

B-52 strikes) were shifted to likely routes of withdrawal and known enemy base camps in the area.

After contact was broken and the enemy routed, the Blue Spaders began to police the battlefield, evacuate casualties, and bury the Viet Cong dead. Four hundred ninety-one bodies were found among their defenses and those of Colonel Lazzell's battalion. After sweeps around the area had been made, the known enemy dead totaled many more. During the two-day battle, the enemy (all three battalions of the 271st Regiment of the 9th Viet Cong Division and elements of the 70th Guard Regiment) lost 609 killed, 5 captured, and over 50 weapons of all types. U.S. casualties were 17 killed and 102 wounded.

During the mortar attack on Fire Support Patrol Base C (where the 2d Brigade command post was located), Colonel Grimsley was wounded and evacuated; command of the brigade was assumed by General Hollingsworth. Later that day, command was turned over to Colonel Haig.

During the fight artillery units of the 1st Division had fired some 15,000 rounds into the battle area, while Air Force jet fighter-bombers logged 103 sorties with over 100 tons of ordnance in support of the ground action.

Asked at what point the pendulum of victory had swung in his favor, Colonel Haig replied:

> In the subjective sense there's no question: with the arrival of the air, tactical air and especially the ordnance, the CBU ordnance was the main factor. However, this is subjective . . . and while it was the straw that broke the camel's back, I would be very remiss if I didn't say that the artillery . . . our mortars, and our own automatic weapons were major factors. And had not all of these been employed to their utmost, and closely coordinated, and well integrated, no single factor by itself would have changed the outcome. . . . As it turned out, the amount of fire that we had falling by way of artillery and our own automatic fire and infantry weapons, [and,] may I add . . . the CBU, with the enemy configured as he was, that is, stacked in depth, in the open, and moving forward, [it was this] combination of things that really made the difference.

Colonel Haig had this further thought about the battle of Ap Gu:

> In this particular attack, I think, as in ATTLEBORO last fall, when you get belly to belly with a large VC force, they are not sufficiently flexible to react especially intelligently. They are going to react like most soldiers and that is to attack. In this case, we were right on their doorstep. We found them by aggressive reconnaissance, the order was called, and the battle was started. . . . I think this was a case of being in their backyard, confronting the commander . . . with a basic problem: When the enemy [the U.S. force] is there, do you run? If you run on top of the series of defeats, where do you stop? When do your men finally realize this is a lost cause? I think this commander was confronted with that very tough decision and he came down hard on the wrong side—at least from the perspective of his future effectiveness.

Back near the Cambodian border that Viet Cong commander probably would have agreed.

CHAPTER XIV

Phase III—Termination

Phase II of JUNCTION CITY came to a close on 15 April. The original intention was that the operation would then cease; however, the first two phases had proved so successful that Phase III was initiated. Control of this last phase was to be the sole responsibility of the 25th Infantry Division, which would commit a brigade to it.

Phase III continued the objectives of JUNCTION CITY I and II, using the mobile brigade concept to conduct offensive operations in War Zone C. The 3d Brigade, 4th Division, had already relieved the 196th Brigade of these operations near the end of Phase II. Therefore when the final phase opened, the 3d of the 4th continued to secure the towns of Tay Ninh and Suoi Da and Route 26 south from Tay Ninh, and to operate throughout the lower western half of War Zone C. One battalion of the brigade conducted search and destroy operations north of Route 247, thereby affording a degree of protection for the completion of the Special Forces camp at Prek Klok. The brigade was deployed until 20 April, when it ended its participation in JUNCTION CITY.

On the 21st the 1st Brigade, 9th Division, with a tank company and the South Vietnamese 36th Ranger Battalion attached, came under the operational control of the 25th Division and assumed the mission of the 3d Brigade, 4th Division. For the next twenty days the brigade forces conducted operations throughout the area, but the organized enemy units became almost impossible to find. Most of the contacts made were with relatively small Viet Cong groups; however, many bunkers and military structures were located and destroyed. Casualties sustained by friendly forces were primarily caused by mines and booby traps. It soon became evident that the enemy had dispersed to a new area.

At midnight on 14 May 1967, Operation JUNCTION CITY, the largest military offensive operation of the Vietnamese conflict to that time, was brought to a close.

The statistical results of JUNCTION CITY are impressive. All the regiments of the 9th Viet Cong Division had been trounced. The final totals carried 2,728 enemy killed and 34 prisoners taken.

DROPPING SUPPLIES 40 KILOMETERS NORTH OF TAY NINH CITY

PHASE III—TERMINATION

There were 139 *Chieu Hoi* ralliers and 65 detainees. Among items of equipment captured were 100 crew-served weapons, 491 individual weapons, and thousands of rounds of ammunition, grenades, and mines. More than 5,000 bunkers and military structures were destroyed. Over 810 tons of rice and nearly 40 tons of other foodstuffs such as salt and dried fish were uncovered. Nearly one-half million pages of assorted documents were taken. American personnel losses were 282 killed and 1,576 wounded, while U.S. materiel losses included the destruction of 3 tanks, 21 armored personnel carriers, 12 trucks, 4 helicopters, 5 howitzers, and 2 quad-.50 machine guns and carriers.

In addition to these losses, the enemy suffered other serious setbacks. He had to take time to regroup, refit, reorganize, and receive replacements. Disruption of the headquarters of the Central Office of South Vietnam caused its forces to withdraw to Cambodia and affected its control over Viet Cong activity. Coupled with the loss of large quantities of important documents and the destruction of many important installations and communication networks, this disruption led to a reversal in planning and control during this period and for some time to come. But probably one of the most far-reaching effects of all upon the enemy was the realization that his bases, even in the outer reaches of War Zone C, were no longer havens.

From a psychological standpoint, the enemy in War Zone C was a more difficult target than that normally encountered in the III Corps area. The reason was that the target was composed primarily of hard-core North Vietnamese and Viet Cong; as a result, the usual *Chieu Hoi* propaganda appeals based on family hardship and separation were not so effective as they were with guerrilla-type units. Early in the operation, quick reaction was recognized as the key to the successful psychological exploitation of hard-core targets.

Commenting on this aspect of the operation, General Weyand had this to say in his Commander's Evaluation of JUNCTION CITY:

> During JUNCTION CITY we dropped 9,768,000 leaflets and made 102 hours of aerial loudspeaker appeals. The major engagements of 20, 21 and 31 March were followed up with a wide variety of "quick-reaction" leaflets. They showed photographs of VC dead and contained surrender appeals to the survivors. A specially designed memorandum addressed to the CG of the 9th VC Div was reproduced and distributed as a leaflet to further exploit our success of 20 March. A newsletter exploiting VC casualties and explaining the role of our forces was distributed throughout the III CTZ.
>
> Our military civic action projects supported the overall PSYOP effort. They added credibility to our central propaganda theme: The Viet Cong/North Vietnamese Army destroy; the Government of Vietnam/United

ARMORED PERSONNEL CARRIERS *piled high with rice captured from the Viet Cong.*

States/Free World Military Armed Forces help the people. Civic action projects completed by our units in villages and hamlets along the JUNCTION CITY LOC (line of communication) included seven road bridges . . . five kilometers of roads, five wells, and two floating docks. In addition, we repaired five road bridges, thirty footbridges . . . four hospitals, one market place . . . eleven kilometers of roads, six schools, three wells, one village water pump and one village power generator. A total of 59,690 patients were treated under the MEDCAP (medical Civic Action Program) II Program; and we distributed 295,041 pounds of food and clothing to local GVN officials who gave them to needy families.

Our success in this endeavor is evidenced by the fact that 139 Hoi Chanh (Chieu Hoi returnees) were induced to rally despite the hard-core nature of the target audience. The intensive use of PSYOP and Civic Action techniques, coupled with our relentless tactical pressure against the VC, was responsible for the large number of ralliers.

The mission assigned II Field Force for JUNCTION CITY had been to conduct a major operation into War Zone C to destroy COSVN and Viet Cong and North Vietnamese forces and installations. All objectives were accomplished in considerable degree with the exception of the destruction of COSVN forces. In his evaluation of

PHASE III—TERMINATION

the operation, General Hay of the Big Red One set forth some of the reasons for this failure.

Several factors contributed:
The proximity of a privileged sanctuary to the reported locations of COSVN and Headquarters, 9th VC Division.
The extreme difficulty of establishing a seal with sufficient troop density to deny infiltration routes to VC units thoroughly familiar with the dense jungle terrain.
The difficulty of gaining complete surprise, as a result of extensive repositioning of troops and logistical support prior to D-Day, in spite of the efforts devoted to deception measures.

Looking back many months after JUNCTION CITY ended, General Westmoreland, in his *Report on the War in Vietnam*, summarized the effect of the operation in this fashion:

(In addition to the enemy losses) we constructed three airfields capable of handling C-130's, erected a bridge entering (War Zone C) on its eastern edge, cleared innumerable helicopter landing zones, and fortified two camps in which Special Forces teams with CIDG garrisons remained as we withdrew. Henceforth, we would be able to enter this important but difficult area with relative ease and with much smaller forces . . . .
An inviolate Viet Cong stronghold for many years, War Zone C was now vulnerable to allied forces any time we choose to enter.
General Giap portrayed JUNCTION CITY as a "big victory" rather than the serious defeat it was. The North Vietnamese continued to perpetuate the myth of crippling U.S. losses and defeat. This time, if anything, the reports were more exaggerated than usual. According to official North Vietnamese reports, 13,500 allied soldiers were killed in JUNCTION CITY. . . . The enemy claimed 993 vehicles destroyed (800 of them armored) and the destruction of 119 allied artillery pieces. . . . Exaggeration of this magnitude by the enemy was a commonplace. Whether self-deception or carefully contrived myth, its existence played an important part in future decisions the enemy was to make . . . .

However, General Giap's glowing account of victory was belied by high-level defectors a year later as they revealed the full impact of JUNCTION CITY upon the enemy:

They commented—and captured documents confirmed—that the operation was essentially an enemy "disaster." According to these knowledgeable defectors, the loss of major base areas and the resulting deterioration of local forces in III Corps forced the enemy high command to make basic revisions in tactics. JUNCTION CITY convinced the enemy command that continuing to base main force units in close proximity to the key population areas would be increasingly foolhardy. From that time on the enemy made increasing use of Cambodian sanctuaries for his bases, hospitals, training centers, and supply depots.

A turning point in the war had been reached.

Epilogue

This monograph about events in early 1967 has been written in retrospect after four and a half years; I found the view somewhat fuzzy. However, I also found that by immersing myself in the references available it was possible to refresh my memory considerably. Therefore, even with the aberrations which may result from the passage of time, I believe that the following observations concerning CEDAR FALLS and JUNCTION CITY are valid.

Building upon the experience gained in slapping together Operation ATTLEBORO while on the move, CEDAR FALLS–JUNCTION CITY confirmed that we could utilize large quantities of all types of available forces, weapons, and equipment in a successful, co-ordinated operation against large enemy main force units. These operations also confirmed the ATTLEBORO experience that such multidivisional operations have a place in modern counterinsurgency warfare. Thus it was that at the time the enemy believed he had the third and last phase of his planned aggression successfully under way—beginning with the battle of Binh Gia two years earlier—he now found himself facing even larger forces than he could assemble

CEDAR FALLS–JUNCTION CITY also revealed that it was possible to plan for such large operations while maintaining a fairly high degree of secrecy about them. They also confirmed that properly planned and implemented cover and deception operations could permit the prepositioning of forces for the main operation without tipping our hand as to the size, location, or even the possibility of that operation.

The intelligence which was developed prior to these operations was impressive in its accuracy. Not only was it generally correct concerning the activities of major enemy elements, it was also quite accurate with respect to the location of installations and facilities. Of the 177 separate enemy facilities uncovered by the 11th Armored Cavalry Regiment during CEDAR FALLS, 156 (88 percent) were located within 500 meters of the site shown in intelligence holdings before the operation. The average distance error was 200 meters. During JUNCTION CITY the accuracy was slightly less than 40 percent located within 500 meters of their predicted sites—still a respectable figure. Thus both operations lent credibility to the system of pattern activity analysis.

The engineer support which was provided during CEDAR FALLS–JUNCTION CITY was typical of that which I observed during my entire tour in Vietnam: outstanding. I found that there was never any mission too difficult for the engineer commands. Even by mid-1966 our engineers had changed the face of Vietnam; I can imagine how it must appear now. During CEDAR FALLS and JUNCTION CITY the tasks undertaken—many of them extremely difficult—were made to look easy.[1] The success of the jungle-destruction operation using Rome Plows, bulldozers, and tankdozers was particularly impressive. However, the discouraging aspect of such operations is that it takes but a short time for the jungle to grow again. After all, the clearing operation does not completely eliminate the jungle by digging it out by its roots; rather it cuts it off a short distance above the ground. Once the jungle has been cut, some system must be devised to keep it from growing back; otherwise, it must be cut again and again.

Another outstanding aspect of CEDAR FALLS–JUNCTION CITY was the close air support provided by the Air Force; it was typical of the support the Air Force always gave the Big Red One, the only outfit for which I can speak authoritatively. The short reaction time; the intense desire by the forward air controller—and the pilots of the flight he was directing—to put the ordnance exactly on the spot desired by the ground commander; the ability to lay down cluster bomb unit runs within thirty meters of friendly forces in order to cause the enemy to break contact; and the ability to bring in air strikes at night under artifical illumination where one slight mistake in depth perception meant "so long" were all capabilities which left a lasting impression upon us infantrymen. Surely there were occasions when the flights arrived over the target without the kind of ordnance requested, but not often. I could not be more outspoken in my praise for the professionalism displayed by the supporting Air Force personnel.

One of the unsung heroes of CEDAR FALLS–JUNCTION CITY was the logistical arm which kept us in food, clothing, ammunition, gas, weapons, medical supplies—everything we consumed or used.

---

[1] If our military system has taught us anything over the years it is that a command is a reflection of its commander. There is no question in my mind but that the 1st Engineer Battalion of the 1st Division, the engineer unit whose operations I observed most, accomplished the myriad tasks which faced it in so professional a manner largely because of its commander, Colonel Kiernan. He had graduated number one in his West Point class, was a big strapping man, had a "can do" additude and an infectious sense of humor, and figured there was nothing which he and his command could not do—and he was right. These characteristics permeated his command and made it what surely must have been the finest engineer outfit in Vietnam among many which were outstanding. (Colonel Kiernan met a tragic death when his helicopter skid caught a high-tension wire as it flew low under the flight pattern of Bien Hoa airport, just seven days before he was to return home.)

Logistical troops repaired our damaged equipment, evacuated our dead and wounded. The operations were the largest ever supported, and they extended over greater distances. During Phase I a forward logistical operations control center was established at Tay Ninh with the primary mission of controlling three forward support areas located at Trai Bi, the French Fort, and Suoi Da. At Minh Thanh the Big Red One established a forward support element and the 1st Brigade, 9th Division, received its supplies at Lai Khe. On five days of the first week of Phase I, the 173d Brigade and the 25th Division received airdrops. During that phase a trailer transfer point was established at Tay Ninh which permitted the five-ton tractors from Saigon–Long Binh depots to drop their loaded trailers and return to the depots with empties. During Phase II the regular Tay Ninh Supply Point took care of the 25th Division units while a forward support area was established at Quan Loi. From 21 March to 7 April the 196th Brigade was supported primarily by airdrop. Also during Phase II it was found possible to "throughput" artillery ammunition from the Long Binh Ammunition Supply Dump directly to the fire support bases, resulting in considerable savings in personnel, material handling equipment, transportation, and time. (The throughput operation also was quite exciting to the drivers and their "shotguns.") Except for resupplying the units at Minh Thanh by air, daily resupply from Saigon–Long Binh during Phase II was by truck, with airlift backup available in an emergency.

On occasion there were hitches in the logistics system, but, from my observation, they were few and far between. The logisticians should take pride in their performance.

Operations CEDAR FALLS and JUNCTION CITY confirmed in the minds of most of us the decisive role played by artillery and air during major battles such as those fought with the 9th Viet Cong Division. They also verified the need to get as much firepower as possible on an attacking enemy without delay and, in this regard, to establish a fire co-ordination line and use artillery and air strikes simultaneously. Again these operations verified the need to have artillery fire (preferably 105-mm., because of its rapid rate of fire) available to support any unit, regardless of size, when operating in an area in which contact with the enemy is possible. Further, CEDAR FALLS and JUNCTION CITY again showed us the wisdom of having fire support bases mutually supporting.

There has always been much discussion about the type of fighting position one should require his men to dig and the manner in which a night defensive position should be organized. Different commanders have varying ideas, and a position for the flat terrain found in most of the III Corps zone might not be the proper one for use in the Central Highlands. However, those of us in the Big Red One were convinced that the "DePuy" fighting position[2] was right for us. That position called for a hole deep enough for a man to stand in with his helmet on, with full overhead cover reinforced by logs or steel rods, properly camouflaged, with two firing ports, each set at a 45-degree angle from a line directly to the front. An enemy weapon firing at the front of the fighting position could not hit a firing port, but struck the thick berm in front. Each individual fighting position was so placed that it could mutually support the positions on either side. Thus, the night defensive position was mutually supporting all around with interlocking fires. (Our soldiers didn't stop digging and building until their positions were finished.) The value of this concept was proved during the heavy mortar, rocket, and recoilless rifle attack at the outset of the battle of Ap Gu on 1 April. Everyone was in his fighting position and only twelve men were wounded during the shelling.

The experience of the 3d Brigade, 4th Division, on 19 March, when it went into a "hot" landing zone with unfortunate results, supported the contention of many of us that, unless there are civilians in the area, troops should never be brought into a landing zone on an airmobile assault unless the zone and surrounding area have been covered by an artillery and air strike preparation. As mentioned above, the use of bombs with instantaneous fuzes was also essential for those specific areas in the landing zone where the lift helicopters would touch down in order to cut the wires leading to command-detonated explosives.

With respect to the enemy contacted during the two operations, we found most of them dedicated, well-disciplined, persistent, tenacious, and courageous, often displaying more "guts" than sense. It was a sheer physical impossibility to keep him from slipping away whenever he wished if he were in terrain with which he was familiar—generally the case. The jungle is usually just too thick and too widespread to hope ever to keep him from getting away; thus the option to fight was usually his. We also found it very difficult to prevent him from mining the roads at night. The routes were just too extensive for the number of troops available. We could not expect our men to outpost the roads all night and beat the jungle on search and destroy all day. We restorted to nightly "thunder runs" in which a small armored detachment ran down stretches of road at different times on different nights trying to discourage mining. Before using the routes the next day, mine

---

[2] Named for Major General (now Lieutenant General) William E. DePuy, then commanding general of the 1st Infantry Division, who designed it.

clearing teams swept them; then they were outposted, with search and destroy operations away from the roads.

One could not help but wonder about the efficacy of the enemy's intelligence system in light of his attacks during Phases I and II, particularly the ones on 10 and 20 March against mechanized and cavalry units on the perimeters. To many of us these attacks seemed stupid. However, looking at the international scene, it may well have been that Hanoi wished to score a major victory about the time of the Guam Conference between President Lyndon B. Johnson and officials of the South Vietnamese government held on 20–21 March. Having failed in his endeavors on 10, 20, and 21 March, it appeared that out of sheer desperation he tried one more time to chalk up a victory at Ap Gu on 1 April. From these four battles he should have learned that if his attack is not successful enough to overrun the defensive position in the first few minutes, he risks being decimated by artillery and air strikes.

One of the discouraging features of both CEDAR FALLS and JUNCTION CITY was the fact that we had insufficient forces, either U.S. or South Vietnamese, to permit us to continue to operate in the Iron Triangle and War Zone C and thereby prevent the Viet Cong from returning. In neither instance were we able to stay around, and it was not long before there was evidence of the enemy's return. Only two days after the termination of CEDAR FALLS, I was checking out the Iron Triangle by helicopter and saw many persons who appeared to be Viet Cong riding bicycles or wandering around on foot. We set up some Eagle flights from our division cavalry squadron and went in, set up roadblocks, and picked up thirty-one men who were suspect. One of our choppers was fired upon as it went in. Later in the day we found some Viet Cong hiding in the extreme southeastern part of the triangle along the Thi Tinh River; they made the mistake of firing upon us.

During the cease-fire for *Tet*, 8–12 February, the Iron Triangle was again literally crawling with what appeared to be Viet Cong. They could be seen riding into, out of, and within the triangle. Finally, in frustration, I was able to get the South Vietnamese civilian officials to set up some checkpoints at appropriate places to monitor identification and proper documentation. There was a definite lack of enthusiasm on the part of the South Vietnamese to do such things during *Tet;* however, we did discourage the enemy from flaunting his *Tet* freedom in our faces. Periodic reconnaissance of the triangle confirmed Viet Cong activity within it. When warranted, artillery and air strikes were brought in to engage them and discourage their activities.

EPILOGUE 159

During Phase I of JUNCTION CITY the 1st Engineers went to great effort to build the airfield capable of handling C-130's at Katum, just south of the Cambodian border; when that phase ended we packed up and left the airfield unsecured, expecting to use it the next time we went into that area (after checking it for mines and other devices). It did not take the enemy long to start mining it. Overflying the airstrip one week after the end of Phase I, we could count about twenty-five holes dug in and around the laterite strip and, through binoculars, could see what appeared to be demolition material lying near the holes.

In order to discourage the enemy from having complete freedom in War Zone C again, General Westmoreland had intended to use the 196th Brigade as a "floating brigade" to conduct mobile operations in the Phase I area. However, the situation in I Corps area compelled him to withdraw the 196th in April and send it north. Reconnaissance flights over War Zone C following JUNCTION CITY revealed that the enemy was returning.

These two operations provided what might be called missed opportunities when evaluated in terms of what might have been if the commander could have written his own ticket; that is, had there been no constraints on time and forces available. For example, had we stayed in the CEDAR FALLS operation longer we could have rooted out more Viet Cong, received more ralliers, cut down more jungle, and destroyed more enemy facilities and installations. In JUNCTION CITY it appeared to some that at the beginning of Phase II, since we had already operated in the western half of War Zone C and had troops on the west at the end of Phase I, we should have made our push from west to east against a blocking force along the Saigon River. Or we could have left a blocking force along Route 4 from Prek Klok to Katum and on northeast to the Cambodian border; our Phase II operation could then have pushed west against it. Another missed opportunity came as an aftermath to the battle of Ap Gu. Had forces been made available, they could have air assaulted into landing zones along the Cambodian border to block the withdrawal of the 271st Viet Cong Regiment as the 1st Battalion, 16th Infantry, and 1st Battalion, 2d Infantry, pursued them. But a discussion of missed opportunities is akin to Monday morning quarterbacking and probably has about the same validity.

The most lasting impression I have of these two operations—in fact of all my Vietnam tour—is of the magnificent American soldier who made them possible. Shortly after my return from Vietnam I had occasion to express my feelings about that soldier in a speech given on 19 October 1967 at the Yorktown Day celebration in Yorktown, Virginia. I find those words still appropriate to describe the soldier who fought in CEDAR FALLS and JUNCTION CITY.

. . . who is this American soldier in Vietnam? He is a boy, about 19 years of age, armed and in uniform, who did not choose to be there. He would have preferred to remain at home, comfortable, enjoying the many attractions and conveniences available to Americans; secure in the company of his family, his friends, his sweetheart. Thoughts of those persons at home creep into his mind, even at times when he is trying to force himself to concentrate on the battle at hand. And in the jungles and rice paddies of Vietnam, this smooth-cheeked, bright-eyed, enthusiastic boy becomes a man. He lives with fear, he lives with carnage, he lives with death. Burned forever into his memory are ugly sights and awesome sorrows which at times are almost too much for a boy, just turned man, to bear. He kills the enemy but questions the waste and folly of war. He sees his buddy killed beside him and asks why? Why was it his turn to go today and not mine? He exults in the victories won by his outfit, but he weeps with grief while attending the memorial services for his buddies who fell in the fight. He understands the cause for which he is fighting; his enthusiasm, dedication and motivation are contagious. He looks with disgust at reports of those back home who question his being and fighting in the far-off place. He dismisses such reports with a shrug, remarking "Those guys back home just don't know what it's all about."

You will see your soldier in Vietnam digging his defensive fighting position in a driving monsoon rain, up to his waist in water and mud, stopping occasionally to bail out the position with his helmet. Or you will find him combating the heat and misery of the jungle floor. But whatever the conditions, he will greet you with a big smile and reassure you: "Don't worry about this position; we'll be ready; the Viet Cong will never take it."

That's your soldier in Vietnam today, a man, who knowing he has 12 months to serve in that country, has resolved to do an outstanding job for that period. To match his spirit, his courage, his determination, enthusiasm and devotion with a comparable level of decisiveness, judgment, imagination and know-how is a challenge to every leader in Vietnam.

Glossary

ABILINE	April 1966 allied operation conducted east of Saigon as a spoiling operation against an enemy move on the capital
AK47	Soviet-designed and manufactured assault rifle, 7.62 mm.
APC	Armored personnel carrier
ARVN	Army of the Republic of Vietnam
ATTLEBORO	Operation resulting in a battle that took place September–November 1966 northwest of Saigon
AVLB	Armored vehicle launched bridge
Bailey bridge	Standard Army military bridge using prefabricated steel panels
beehive round	Canisters filled with hundreds of metal darts
the Big Red One	U.S. 1st Infantry Division
BIRMINGHAM	April 1966 operation in which the U.S. 1st Infantry Division moved into War Zone C, uncovering great quantities of supplies
the Blackhorse Regiment	U.S. 11th Armored Cavalry Regiment
the Blue Spaders	Men of the 1st Battalion, U.S. 26th Infantry
Buddy operations	Operations by combined U.S. and South Vietnamese forces
CBU	Cluster bomb units
Chieu Hoi program	The "open arms" program initiated by President Diem in April 1963 promising clemency and financial aid to guerrillas who stopped fighting and returned to live under government authority
Chinook	CH–47 helicopter
claymore mine	A shaped, antipersonnel mine which when detonated propels small steel cubes in a fan-shaped pattern
cordon and search	Operation to seal off and search an area
COSVN	Central Office of South Vietnam
CS	Riot control agent
dozer-infantry team	A team of tankdozers, bulldozers, Rome

	Plows, and infantry which cut into the jungle
Eiffel bridge	Nonstandard metal military bridge of French design
EL PASO II	A series of operations conducted in June and July 1966 by the U.S. 1st Infantry Division and the Vietnamese 5th Division on the eastern flank of War Zone C
elm(s)	Element(s)
FITCHBURG	January 1967 operation in preparation for CEDAR FALLS
FSB	Fire support base
FSPB	Fire support patrol base
G-3	Assistant Chief of Staff, Operations
GADSDEN	Original name for Operation JUNCTION CITY, later designating one of the deception operations in the first phase of JUNCTION CITY
GVN	The government of the Republic of Vietnam
Huey	UH-ID helicopter
IIFFORCEV	II Field Force, Vietnam
the Iron Brigade	3d Brigade, U.S. 1st Infantry Division
J-2	Assistant Chief of Staff, Intelligence
KIA	Killed in action
local force	Viet Cong combat unit subordinate to a district or province
LTL	Vietnamese interprovincial route
LZ	Landing zone
M16	U.S. lightweight, rapid-firing 5.56-mm. rifle
M60	U.S. 7.62-mm. machine gun
M79	Shoulder-fired weapon employing an explosive 40-mm. grenade-type round
MACV	U.S. Military Assistance Command, Vietnam
mad minute	Concentrated fire of all weapons for a specified time at optimum rate
main force elements	Viet Cong and North Vietnamese military units subordinate to the Central Office of South Vietnam, military regions, or other higher echelons of command

GLOSSARY

marching fire	Fire delivered by infantry in an assault, especially with rifle fired from the hip or rapidly from the shoulder
MEDCAP	Medical Civic Action Program
meeting engagement	Collision between two advancing forces, neither of which is fully deployed for battle
NDP	Night defensive position
NIAGARA FALLS	Cover operation designed to place combat elements in position for CEDAR FALLS before striking the main blow
NVA	North Vietnam Army
OA	Objective area
pattern activity analysis	Procedure begun in mid-1966 which consisted of detailed plotting on maps of information on enemy activity obtained from a variety of sources over an extended period of time
pods	Rubberized 500-gallon containers used to hold bulk Class III products
PSYOP	Psychological operations
QL	Vietnamese national route
quad-.50	Four heavy machine guns that traverse from a single pedestal and which are fired simultaneously by one gunner
RAG	River Assault Group (Vietnamese)
RPG2	Small Soviet-made bazooka-type antitank grenade launcher
S–3	Operations and training officer
search and clear	Offensive military operation designed to sweep through an area with the mission of locating, driving out, or destroying the enemy
search and destroy	Offensive operations designed to seek out and destroy enemy forces, headquarters, and supply installations, with emphasis on destruction rather than re-establishment of government control
"Spooky"	C–47 aircraft with two 7.62-mm. Gatling-type guns and illumination flares
Task Force ALPHA	1st and 5th South Vietnamese Marine Battal-

	ions under the control of the U.S. 25th Division for Phase I of JUNCTION CITY
Task Force DEANE	U.S. 173d Airborne Brigade during Operation NIAGARA FALLS
Task Force WALLACE	Two South Vietnamese units (35th Ranger Battalion and one troop from the 3d Battalion, 1st Cavalry) which augmented the U.S. 1st Division in Phase I of JUNCTION CITY
TL	Vietnamese provincial route
Tropic Lightning Division	U.S. 25th Infantry Division
TUCSON	Deception operation conducted to position forces and materiel for JUNCTION CITY
VC	Viet Cong

Index

A Go Noi (1): 46
ABILENE: 5
Accidents, combat: 112-13
Agents, employment of: 17
Air blowers, tactical use: 72-73
Air defense, enemy: 17
Air operations. *See* Tactical air support.
Air strikes. *See* Tactical air support.
Air units, Army. *See* Helicopters.
Airborne Battalions:
   1st, 503d Brigade: 45-46
   2d, 503d Brigade: 45-50, 55, 73, 101
   4th, 503d Brigade: 45, 55
Airborne Brigades
   1st, 101st Division: 84, 87
   173d: 11, 22-23, 28-29, 31, 46, 71, 84, 87, 97, 100-111, 123, 125-26, 128, 156
Airdrops. *See* Airlifts of troops and supplies; Parachute assaults.
Airfield construction: 83, 87, 90, 106-107, 112, 119, 122-23, 126, 153, 159
Airlifts of troops and supplies: 2, 12, 23, 27, 29-31, 34, 47, 112, 120, 127, 140, 156
Airmobile assaults: 8, 11, 23, 30-31, 34-36, 38, 42-45, 54, 64-66, 83, 93, 96, 100-102, 104-106, 109-10, 122, 124, 126, 135-37, 142, 157, 159
ALA MOANA: 55
Alcala, Captain Raoul H.: 129-34
Ambush actions: 26, 47-49, 77, 119, 129-32, 142-43
Ambush actions, enemy: 5, 7, 17, 127, 133
Ammunition supply: 47, 112, 120, 138, 156
Amphibious operations. *See* Republic of Vietnam Navy.
An Loc: 7, 23, 85, 90, 107, 122
Ap Bau Bang: 123, 128-35
Ap Cha Do: 135
Ap Gu: 124, 128, 140-48, 157-59
Armor units: 18, 22-23, 100, 103, 127, 129-33, 139-40, 149
Armored Battalions, 2d, 34th Armor: 46, 139-40
Armored Cavalry Regiment, 11th: 18, 22, 28-29, 31, 44, 55, 60-61, 87, 100-11, 123-24, 154

Armored personnel carriers: 74, 119-20, 129-33, 151
Arsenals, enemy: 93
Artillery Bases
   I: 29, 71, 102, 114, 120, 126
   II: 112, 114, 118, 120
   III: 120
Artillery Battalions
   2d, 33d Artillery: 114, 119
   2d, 77th Artillery: 136-40
   3d, 319th Artillery: 101
   7th, 9th Artillery: 129
Artillery fire support: 30, 37, 42-43, 77-78, 93, 100, 103, 110, 114-16, 119-20, 131, 134-35, 137n, 138-44, 146-48, 156-58
Atrocities, enemy: 3, 5, 85-86
ATTLEBORO: 1, 4, 8-12, 83, 85, 135, 148, 154
Aviation Battalion, 1st: 35

Base camps: 64, 83, 90, 112, 119, 122-23, 126, 149, 153
Base camps, enemy: 27, 42, 44, 68, 70, 84, 86, 95-96, 104, 106-107, 151
Bau Bang: 131
Bau Long: 84, 94, 96
Baumann, Lieutenant Colonel Lewis R.: 44
Beehive rounds: 138-39
Ben Cat: 15, 23, 29, 31, 44, 58, 60-61, 64, 86
Ben Cat District: 75
Ben Co: 27
Ben Suc: 15, 23, 25, 29, 31, 34-42, 44, 55, 58-59, 78
Bender, Lieutenant Colonel John A.: 136
Bien Hoa: 29, 31, 101, 126
Binh Duong: 34
Binh Gia: 5, 154
Binh Long Province: 84, 94-95
BIRMINGHAM: 7, 15, 83
Black Virgin Mountain (Nui Ba Den): 11, 86, 118, 127
Blocking Positions
   YANKEE: 25
   ZULU: 29
Bo Tuc: 109-10, 124
Boi Loi woods: 25-26, 35

Booby traps, enemy: 22, 37, 42, 51, 78, 149
Bothwell, Sergeant Frank: 48–49
Bridge construction, destruction, and repair: 17, 60–61, 86, 90, 103–104, 122–23, 152–53
Brown, Sergeant Julius: 49
Brownlee, Lieutenant Colonel Robert W.: 45–46
Buddhists: 3
Buffalo turbine: 73
Bulldozers: 62, 155. *See also* Land-clearing operations.
Bung Cong: 34
Bunker systems: 38, 40, 42, 47, 51–52, 55, 59, 70, 72, 74, 78, 93, 110, 149, 151

Cachua Forestry Reserve: 35–36
Caldwell, Colonel William B.: 94, 100, 123
Cambodia: 7, 11, 83, 85–87, 91–93, 97–101, 105–106, 110, 124, 140, 142, 148, 151, 153, 159
Camouflage, enemy: 54, 115
Capital Military District, Republic of Vietnam: 77
Carlile, Major Cecil O.: 35
Carney, Captain Thomas P.: 47, 49
Castro, Staff Sergeant Frank P.: 34
Casualties
 enemy: 7, 12, 30, 36–37, 46, 52, 54, 70, 74, 79, 93, 96, 106, 108–11, 116, 121, 128, 135, 140, 143, 147, 149
 Republic of Vietnam: 5, 74
 United States: 12, 30, 37, 66, 74, 94, 96, 103, 106, 108–109, 112, 116, 119, 121, 131–35, 137, 140, 143–44, 147, 151
Cattle, enemy use of: 129
Cau Dinh: 28
Cavalry Squadrons:
 1st, 4th Cavalry: 46, 55, 59–60, 72
 3d, 4th Cavalry: 52
 3d, 5th Cavalry: 96, 129–35
Central Highlands: 157
Central Office of South Vietnam (COSVN): 2–3, 12, 77, 83–84, 87, 90–91, 93, 103, 106, 108–10, 126, 151–53
Chemical Detachment, 242d: 60
Chemical weapons, use of: 54, 60, 68, 71–73
Chieu Hoi program: 30, 56, 74, 76, 78, 93, 106, 151–52
Chon Thanh: 95
Civic actions: 37–38, 46, 52–53, 151–52

Civilian Irregular Defense Groups, Republic of Vietnam: 87, 90, 112, 119, 122–23, 126, 153
Civilians, evacuation and housing: 23, 29, 34, 38–40, 58–59, 74, 77, 79
Clothing distribution: 152
Cluster bomb units: 52, 114, 134, 146–48, 155
Cobb, Colonel William W.: 31, 100, 123
Collins, Lieutenant Colonel Edward J.: 118–19
Combat Aviation Group, 12th: 24
Combat units. *See* Ground forces.
Communications, combat: 115, 131
Communications, enemy: 67
Cordon-and-search tactics: 76
Corps Tactical Zones
 I: 127, 159
 III: 17–18, 22–24, 78–79, 87, 151, 153, 157
Cu Chi: 23, 30, 55
Cundiff, Captain Brian H.: 146

Danger Forward: 113, 118
Daniel, Lieutenant Colonel Charles D.: 119
Dau Tieng: 11, 29, 31, 35, 85, 97, 127
Davis, Sergeant First Class Kenneth D.: 119
Deadline rates: 65
Deane, Brigadier General John R., Jr.: 28, 100–101, 123. *See also* Task Forces: DEANE.
Defoliation operations: 47, 55
Demolition operations: 38, 40–41, 68–69
Dental services: 38
DePuy, Major General William E.: 11–12, 24, 39, 70, 78, 83, 112, 157
Di An: 29
Diem, Ngo Dinh: 3
Discipline, enemy: 157
Distilleries, enemy: 93
Docks, construction of: 152
Documents captured and destroyed: 10, 12, 17, 30, 46, 50, 52, 54–55, 68–69, 74, 77, 93, 96, 107, 109, 137n, 140, 151
Dorren, Staff Sergeant: 132
Dozer-infantry teams. *See* Land-clearing operations.
Dustoffs. *See* Helicopters: casualties, evacuation by.

Egersdorfer, Captain Rudolf: 38
Eisenhower, Dwight D.: 1

EL PASO II: 7, 10
Engineer Battalions
  1st: 29, 40–41, 60–71, 107, 122, 155n, 159
  168th: 61, 67–68, 119
Engineer Company, 175th: 27
Engineer Group, 79th: 24, 60–61, 65
Engineer operations: 103, 112, 119, 122, 155. *See also* by subject.
Engineer School, Republic of Vietnam: 70
Equipment losses. *See* Materiel losses.
Evacuees. *See* Civilians, evacuation and housing.

Farmer, Private First Class Michael: 49
Festa, First Lieutenant Roger A.: 129–33
Field Force, II: 11, 15–24, 30, 79, 83–90, 97–111, 123, 125, 152
Filhol Plantation: 25–27, 30, 52, 54
Fire power superiority: 156
Fire Support Bases: 156
  20: 129–32
  C: 125, 127, 137n, 140, 144–47
  GOLD: 127, 136–37
  PARRY: 126
  THRUST: 124, 144
Fish, Major George B.: 35
FITCHBURG: 25–29
Flamethrowers, use of: 60, 72
Food
  distribution by U.S.: 152
  enemy losses: 10, 12, 38, 43–44, 46–47, 51–52, 54–56, 60, 71, 74, 77–78, 93, 96, 106–107, 151
Forward air controllers: 115, 138, 155
Foxhole construction: 156–57
France, withdrawal by: 1, 4
French Fort: 102, 110, 115, 126–27, 156
Froelich, Colonel V. W., USAF: 107n
Fuller, Colonel Marvin D.: 27, 100

GADSDEN: 84–87, 91–94
Garth, Colonel Marshall B.: 91, 94, 100, 127, 136
Gaura, Private First Class Gary: 49
Geneva Accords: 1
Gia Dinh: 15, 34
Giap, General Vo Nguyen, North Vietnam Army: 153
Gorman, Lieutenant Colonel Paul F.: 134
Grantham, Major Carl R.: 40
Grenade assaults: 47

Grenade assaults, enemy: 108–10, 115, 119–20, 131, 133, 142
Griffin, Staff Sergeant Richard A.: 119–20
Grimsley, Colonel James A.: 31, 147
Ground forces
  commitment to the Republic of Vietnam: 2, 5
  expansion: 5
Guam Conference: 158
Guerrilla operations, enemy: 1–2, 85–86, 93, 129

Haig, Lieutenant Colonel Alexander M.: 31, 140–48
Haszard, Lieutenant Colonel Sidney S.: 131–34
Hawkins, Lieutenant Colonel Alvin S.: 35
Hay, Major General John H., Jr.: 97, 135, 143, 153
Healy, Lieutenant Colonel Michael D.: 45
Helicopters
  assaults by. *See* Airmobile assaults; Tactical air support.
  casualties, evacuation by: 48, 116, 119–20, 134, 140
  commitment to the Republic of Vietnam: 2
  damaged and destroyed: 44, 137, 151
  supply by. *See* Airlifts of troops and supplies.
Highway 4: 87, 97–106, 108, 110, 112–13, 116, 118, 120, 126–27, 159
Highway 13: 7, 28, 84, 86, 94–96, 122–23, 129, 133–34
Highway 14: 67
Highway 22: 97, 103, 108, 110
Highway 26: 87, 149
Highway 239: 87, 95
Highway 242: 95
Highway 244: 123–27
Highway 245: 95–96
Highway 246: 90, 101–102, 107, 109, 122–27
Highway 247: 87, 97, 149
Hill, Private First Class Michael: 49
Hill, First Lieutenant Richard A.: 142–43
Ho Bo woods: 25–26, 30–31, 52, 54
Hoi Chanh. See Chieu Hoi program.
Hollingsworth, Brigadier General James F.: 131, 147
Hospitals, construction of: 152
Hua, Staff Sergeant George: 132

Ice, Major Donald A.: 36
Illumination, battlefield: 52, 110, 131–32, 134, 145, 155
Infantry Battalions
  1st, 2d Infantry: 55, 140–48, 159
  1st, 5th Infantry: 54
  1st, 16th Infantry: 43, 47, 112–17, 143–48, 159
  1st, 26th Infantry: 29, 31, 37, 55, 59, 137n, 140–48
  1st, 27th Infantry: 51–52
  1st, 28th Infantry: 43–44, 64, 135
  2d, 2d Infantry: 43, 112, 118–21, 135n, 139–40
  2d, 12th Infantry: 137–40
  2d, 18th Infantry: 44
  2d, 22d Infantry: 139–40
  2d, 27th Infantry: 53
  2d, 28th Infantry: 43–44, 112
  3d, 22d Infantry: 136–40
Infantry Brigades
  1st, 1st Infantry Division: 94–111, 122–28
  1st, 9th Infantry Division: 97, 100, 122–28, 129–35, 149, 156
  2d, 1st Infantry Division: 28–29, 31, 37–38, 42, 55, 59, 72, 110, 123–24, 140, 145
  2d, 25th Infantry Division: 25, 27, 30, 46, 51, 53, 55, 100–11
  3d, 1st Infantry Division: 28–29, 31, 42–44, 59, 71, 94–96, 100–12, 120, 124
  3d, 4th Infantry Division: 91, 100, 108, 126–28, 136–40, 149, 157
  196th Light: 7–8, 11, 23, 25–30, 46, 53–55, 91, 100, 102, 105, 110, 126–28, 149, 156, 159
Infantry Divisions
  in counterinsurgency operations: 154
  1st: 7, 11, 23–41, 45, 51, 55–59, 61, 68, 71, 78, 83–91, 94–111, 122–29, 131, 135, 137n, 140–48, 155–57
  4th: 11
  9th: 19
  25th: 11, 23–30, 46, 51–55, 84–94, 97–111, 126–28, 149, 156
Infrared devices: 17, 131
Intelligence estimates and operations: 12, 17–19, 38–39, 42, 74–75, 79, 84–86, 91, 93, 95, 109, 135, 140, 154
Intelligence estimates and operations, enemy: 110, 158
Iron Triangle: 5, 15, 18–42, 45, 51–60, 63, 65, 67, 75–76, 78–79, 85, 158

Johnson, Lyndon B.: 158
Johnson, Specialist Four Walter: 48
Joint operations: 27, 52, 77–78
Jones, Captain George A.: 145–46
Jungle clearing. *See* Land-clearing operations.

Katum: 87, 97–100, 102–104, 106–109, 116, 159
Kendall, Colonel Maurice W.: 123
Kiernan, Lieutenant Colonel Joseph M., Jr.: 29, 40, 60, 155n
King, Sergeant Nathaniel: 47–48
Knowles, Brigadier General Richard T.: 26, 54–55, 76–77, 91, 100, 127
Ky, Nguyen Cao: 4

Lai Khe: 29, 31, 65, 97, 112, 122–23, 131, 156
Land-clearing operations: 17, 27, 29, 40, 46, 55, 60–66, 72, 74, 78, 106, 107n, 112, 123, 155
Landing Zone
  BRAVO: 124
  CHARLIE: 124
  construction: 60
  GEORGE: 124, 140–44
Lao Dong: 2–3
Lazzell, Lieutenant Colonel Rufus C.: 43, 112, 143–44
Leaflets, distribution. *See* Psychological operations.
Leonard, Platoon Sergeant Matthew: 116–17
Lessons from Vietnam: 154–60
Lines of communication: 100
Listening posts: 48–49, 119, 142–43, 145
"Little Elephant's Ear:" 110
Lo Go: 83–85, 91–93, 110
Loc Ninh: 85
Logistical Command, 1st: 24
Logistical support: 12, 155–56
Logistical support, enemy: 95
Long Binh: 30, 156
Long Giao: 31
Long Nguyen: 31, 84, 95
Lopez, Private First Class Steve: 132
Loudspeaker appeals: 37, 151

McChristian, Brigadier General Joseph A.: 18–19, 85

Machine guns, types: 47, 49, 70
Maintenance and repair: 65
Maps
  captured from enemy: 54
  preparation and use: 35
Marion, Captain Duane W.: 129
Marks, Colonel Sidney M.: 31, 94, 100, 110, 115–16
Mass, principle of: 76
Materiel losses: 74, 151
Materiel losses, enemy: 7, 10, 12, 17, 30, 36, 38, 43–44, 46-47, 50–51, 54–55, 68, 74, 78–79, 93, 96, 103–104, 106, 108, 111, 116, 121, 128, 135, 140, 151
Mechanized units, employment of: 77, 93–95, 100, 102, 127, 130–40
Medal of Honor award: 117
Medical services: 37–38, 46, 53, 133–34, 152. *See also* Helicopters: casualties, evacuation by.
Medical services, enemy: 93
Melvin, Chief Warrant Officer Howard P.: 101
Michelin Plantation: 5, 84–85, 94, 96
Military Regions, Viet Cong
  III: 23
  IV: 15, 18–19, 46, 50, 54, 69, 74–75, 78
Mines: 47
Mines, enemy: 22, 37, 42, 44, 51, 78, 103, 108, 127, 137, 149, 157–59
Minh Thanh: 94–96, 101, 104, 106, 116, 126, 156
Minh Thanh Plantation: 84
Monitors: 70–71
Monsoons. *See* Weather, effect on operations.
Mortars and mortar assaults: 47, 112, 119, 129, 138, 143–44, 148
Mortars and mortar assaults, enemy: 112, 115, 119–20, 127, 131–32, 137–38, 143–45
Motor vehicle losses: 74, 151

Napalm, combat use: 134
National Liberation Front: 2–3
Naval gunfire support: 2
Newsweek: 54
Nha Viec: 51
NIAGARA FALLS: 25–29, 60–61, 63
Night operations: 26, 35, 48, 52, 142–43, 156–58
Norman, Private First Class Martin: 49

North Vietnam. *See also* Viet Cong.
  aggression in South: 2–3
  war aims: 1
North Vietnamese Army. *See also* Viet Cong.
  combat effectiveness: 2
  commitment to South: 5
  strength: 2
  101st Regiment: 11, 84–85, 116, 135
Nui Ba Den (Black Virgin Mountain); 11, 86, 118, 127

Oberg, Major Robert E.: 36
Office of Civil Operations: 23, 40
Operational Objective Areas
  FAUST: 124
  SIOUX: 124, 140
Opportunities missed: 159
Owens, Captain William B.: 36

Pacification programs: 5
Palmer, Lieutenant General Bruce, Jr.: 123
Parachute assaults: 15, 83–84, 101, 103n
Patrols, ground: 17, 26, 47–49, 53, 114, 137, 142
Patrols, riverine: 71, 77–78
Pattern activity analysis: 17–18, 84, 154
Pendleton, Lieutenant Colonel Elmer D.: 43
Penedo, Specialist Four Abelardo: 133
Petroleum, oil, lubricants (POL) supply: 64–65
Photography, combat use: 17, 35
Phu Cuong: 23, 34, 39, 58, 70, 78
Phu Hoa Dong: 25, 27, 30, 46, 52
Phu Loi: 27, 31
Phu Thuan: 27
Phuoc Tuy Province: 79
Phuoc Vinh: 23, 29
Pinkney, Sergeant Alton B.: 35
Popular Forces, Republic of Vietnam: 17
Postal service, enemy: 93
Power systems, construction of: 152
Prek Klok: 87, 97–100, 102, 105, 108, 110, 112–21, 126–27, 149, 159
Primis, Major Nick J.: 35
Prisoners, enemy: 12, 36, 38–40, 44, 50 56–57, 68, 73–74, 106, 111, 116, 121, 128, 135, 140, 149. *See also Chieu Hoi* program.
Psychological operations: 37, 56–57, 135, 151–52

Psychological operations, enemy: 86, 108–10, 142

Quan Loi: 23, 97, 102, 106, 122–23, 156

Rach Bap: 34, 39, 58, 64, 67
Rach Kien: 34
Rach Son: 26, 54
Radar, combat use: 131
Ramos-Rasario, Staff Sergeant: 132
Rations: 47
Recoilless rifle fire, enemy: 110, 119–20, 131, 133, 137–38, 143
Reconnaissance, aerial: 17, 52, 54–55, 158–59
Reconnaissance, ground: 112–13, 119, 131, 148
Refugees. See Civilians, evacuation and housing.
Regional Forces, Republic of Vietnam: 17, 24
Repair parts. See Maintenance and repair.
Repatriation program. See Chieu Hoi program.
Republic of Vietnam
　political crises: 3–5
　U.S. policy and commitment: 1–2
　U.S. strength: 2, 158
Republic of Vietnam-armed forces, expansion: 5 See also by name.
Republic of Vietnam Army
　airborne units: 77
　casualties: 5, 74
　Ranger units: 5
　1st Airborne Task Force: 40
　1st Military Intelligence Detachment: 38
　3d Battalion, 1st Cavalry: 97
　5th Division: 7, 24–25
　7th Regiment: 5, 25, 52
　35th Ranger Battalion: 46, 97
　36th Ranger Battalion: 137n, 149
Republic of Vietnam Marine Corps: 5, 104–105
Republic of Vietnam Navy: 24, 39, 52, 77–78
Revolutionary Development: 97, 110, 124
Riverine operations: 70–71
Road construction and repair: 39, 60, 74, 103–104, 106
Road nets: 22. See also Highways.
Rocket assaults: 146
Rocket assaults, enemy: 115, 131, 138, 143

Rogers, Specialist Four Astor: 37
Rome plow: 62–63, 155
Routes, See Highways.
Ruses: 19, 22, 25–29, 76, 84–85, 153–54
Russo, Private First Class Joseph: 48

Sa, Le Van: 56–57
Sabotage: 75
Saigon: 5, 7, 15, 18, 34, 54, 75, 78, 104, 156
Saigon River: 15–18, 23–24, 26–27, 30–34, 46, 51–52, 59–60, 70–71, 86, 90, 107, 122, 159
Sampans, actions against: 46, 51–52, 93
Schools, construction of: 152
Schweitzer, Major Robert L.: 39
Seaman, Lieutenant General Jonathan O.: 15–24, 51, 76–79, 83–84, 97, 104–105, 123
Search-and-destroy operations: 8–10, 25–27, 29, 42, 44–46, 51, 53–59, 77, 87, 90–93, 96–100, 103, 106, 110, 112–13, 123–24, 126–27, 140–42, 149, 158
Searchlights. See Illumination, battlefield.
Security measures: 23, 40, 76–77, 84, 100, 154
Security measures, enemy: 83
Seibert, Colonel Donald A.: 123
Sensor devices: 17
Short, First Lieutenant Harlan E.: 129
Sigholtz, Lieutenant Colonel Robert H.: 45, 101
Silencers, use of: 67
Simpson, Lieutenant Colonel William C.: 43, 142
Smoke, tactical use: 35, 47, 72, 114–15
Snipers, enemy: 37, 44, 51, 66, 70, 115, 120
Soldier, tribute to: 159–60
Special Forces, U.S. Army: 2, 7, 11, 83, 87, 90, 110, 112, 119, 122–23, 126, 149, 153
Special Forces Group, 5th: 2, 11
Sroc Con Trang: 122–25, 127, 137n, 140
Stevens, Specialist Four Eugene W.: 129–31
Strategic air support: 2
Suoi Cau: 35
Suoi Da: 7, 11, 87, 102, 104–105, 107n, 112, 116, 120, 126–27, 149, 156
Suoi Samat: 139
Suoi Tre: 127–28, 135–40
Supply losses. See Materiel losses.
Supply systems and operations: 12, 64–65, 71, 85, 123–24

Supply systems and operations, enemy: 31–34, 38, 41–42, 71, 91, 95
Surprise, application of: 34–37, 76, 145, 153

Tactical air support: 2, 10–12, 18, 30–31, 34, 37, 42–43, 77–78, 93, 103–104, 110, 114–16, 120, 132, 134–35, 137n, 138–43, 146, 148, 155–58. *See also* Strategic air support.
Tan Son Nhut: 54, 78
Tan Uyen: 85
Tank losses: 74, 131, 151
Tank units. *See* Armor units.
Tankdozers. *See* Land-clearing operations.
Task Forces
  ALPHA: 100, 104–105
  DEANE: 28–29, 31, 42, 44–46, 55, 59, 74
  OREGON: 127
  WALLACE: 97–100
Tay Ninh: 8, 23, 26, 55, 86–87, 90–91, 97–100, 127, 149, 156
Tay Ninh Military School, Viet Cong: 75
Tay Ninh Province: 7, 11–12, 15, 79, 85, 87
Terrain features: 22, 42, 86, 91, 94–95, 142, 156–57
Terrorism. *See* Atrocities, enemy.
Tet cease-fire: 158
Thanh Dien Forestry Reserve: 15, 19–25, 42, 44–45, 47, 51–59, 64, 67, 71
Thi Tinh River: 15, 23, 25, 28, 30–31, 44, 47, 52, 55, 60–61, 70–71, 158
Thieu, Nguyen Van: 4
Trai Bi: 93, 103–104, 156
Thuan, Brigadier General Phan Quoc, Army of the Republic of Vietnam: 24
Time: 54, 73
Traffic control: 26
Training programs and areas, enemy: 11, 93
Trench systems, enemy: 10, 42, 110
Trickett, Private First Class William: 145
TUCSON: 84–87, 91, 94–96
Tunnel systems: 10, 12, 23, 38, 40–42, 47, 54–55, 59, 66–70, 72, 74, 78–79, 128

Ulm, Captain Donald S.: 113–16
United States Air Force: 71, 103, 155
  Tactical Air Command: 115
  Seventh Air Force: 24
  3d Tactical Fighter Wing: 24
United States Marine Corps: 2

United States Military Assistance Advisory Group, Vietnam: 2
United States Military Assistance Command, Vietnam. *See also* Westmoreland, General William C.
  genesis: 2
  strength. *See* Republic of Vietnam, U.S. strength.

Vam Co Dong: 86
Vann, John: 23
Vessey, Lieutenant Colonel John W., Jr.: 136
Viet Cong. *See also* North Vietnam; North Vietnamese Army.
  combat effectiveness: 2, 157–58
  strength: 2, 4–5
  tactics: 5, 158
  9th Division: 5, 7, 10–12, 79, 84–85, 90, 116, 121, 128–49, 151, 153, 156
  70th Guards Regiment: 91, 93, 140–48
  165th Regiment: 19, 27–28, 30, 34
  271st Regiment: 11, 85, 91, 93, 108, 140–48, 159
  272d Regiment: 5, 11, 19, 85, 91, 95–96, 121, 135–40
  273d Regiment: 11, 85, 129–35
  680th Training Regiment: 91, 93
  Phu Loi Battalion: 19, 29, 74, 95
  1st Battalion: 19, 74
  2d Battalion: 19
  3d Battalion: 19
  7th Battalion: 19, 74
  8th Battalion: 19, 74
  Ben Cat District Company: 95
  61st Company: 34, 74
  63d Company: 29
  U–80 Artillery: 140
Vietnam War, lessons from: 154–60

War Zone C: 5–7, 11, 15, 79, 83–90, 94–95, 105, 107, 122–27, 135, 140, 149, 151–53, 158–59
War Zone D: 5, 95
Water supply: 152
Weapons losses. *See* Materiel losses.
Weather, effect on operations: 22, 83, 86, 91, 140
Westmoreland, General William C.: 15, 18–19, 40, 75, 79, 83–84, 153, 159. *See also* United States Military Assistance Command, Vietnam.

Weyand, Major General Frederick C.: 24, 91, 100, 151
Whitted, Lieutenant Colonel Jack G.: 44
Wild, Colonel Hugh: 107n
Williams, Staff Sergeant Ernest: 37

Wolfe, Second Lieutenant Hiram M., IV: 129–33

Xom Giua: 91–93
Xuan Loc: 22

www.ingramcontent.com/pod-product-compliance
Lightning Source LLC
Chambersburg PA
CBHW070757100426
42742CB00012B/2166